BY CHANCE ALONE

ALONE

The Young Readers' Edition

BY CHANCE ALONE

The Young Readers' Edition

A Remarkable True Story of Courage
and Survival at Auschwitz

MAX EISEN

Adapted for Young Readers by Kathy Kacer

HARPERCOLLINS PUBLISHERS LTD

Published by HarperCollins Publishers Ltd

HarperCollins books may be purchased for educational, business,
or sales promotional use through our Special Markets Department.

HarperCollins Publishers Ltd
Bay Adelaide Centre, East Tower
22 Adelaide Street West, 41st Floor
Toronto, Ontario, Canada
M5H 4E3

www.harpercollins.ca

Library and Archives Canada Cataloguing in Publication

Title: By chance alone : a remarkable true story of courage and survival at Auschwitz /
Max Eisen ; adapted for young readers by Kathy Kacer.
Names: Kacer, Kathy, 1954- author. | Adaptation of (work): Eisen, Max. By chance alone.
Description: The young readers' edition. | Includes bibliographical references.
Identifiers: Canadiana (print) 20240386191 | Canadiana (ebook) 20240390660 | ISBN
9781443469425 (softcover) | ISBN 9781443469432 (ebook)
Subjects: LCSH: Eisen, Max—Juvenile literature. | LCSH: Auschwitz (Concentration camp)—
Biography—Juvenile literature. | LCSH: Jews, Czech—Canada—Biography—Juvenile literature.
| LCSH: Jews—Czechoslovakia—Biography—Juvenile literature. | LCSH: Holocaust
survivors—Biography—Juvenile literature. | LCSH: Holocaust, Jewish (1939-1945)—
Czechoslovakia—Juvenile literature. | LCSH: Nazi concentration camp inmates—Poland—
Oświęcim—Biography—Juvenile literature. | LCGFT: Autobiographies. | LCGFT: Biographies.
Classification: LCC DS135.C97 E375 2024 | DDC j940.53/18092—dc23

Printed and bound in the United States of America

24 25 26 27 28 LBC 5 4 3 2 1

CONTENTS

Dear Reader,

Max, our father, was a survivor of one of history's most brutal crimes.

As you can imagine, such a violent, traumatic event took a heavy toll on those who lived through it.

Like most survivors, Max was left with physical and emotional scars after his liberation and reintegration into post-war society. He suffered grief and anger due to the extent of his loss. However, living through the experiences of the camps had made him resilient and resourceful. He kept moving forward and overcame negative emotions by relying on sound values and skills learned from his family as a boy and by believing in himself. He was still very young at the end of the war and realized he was responsible for making choices about the path his life would take.

The healing occurred in stages, starting with his years at an orphanage in Marienbad and then his emigration to Canada. He became stronger and more purposeful all the time as life unfolded in his new, adopted country.

One of his most important goals in later life was to ensure that youth, in particular, understood the consequences of hatred and intolerance. Max told them there is no freedom without responsibility. Freedom is not to be taken for granted. It must be defended. In a society where free speech is practised, there will always be those who preach hate. Therefore, hate must be challenged whenever and wherever it occurs.

Max knew from personal experience that even seemingly cultured and law-abiding democracies can descend into chaos and destruction. One person can have an impact in safeguarding rights and freedoms, but it is the multiplied influence of many determined, like-minded individuals that will keep society safe from oppression.

When Max spoke to a classroom of students, he would always drive home the message to be an "upstander" for freedom and not a "bystander," and to confront the hateful offender by saying, "We will not allow you to bully others . . . not in our school, not in our town, not in our country."

His words were passed on to his family and those who heard him speak. His aim? To inform us and to steer us toward a path of mutual respect and cohesion.

Ed and Larry Eisen

BY CHANCE ALONE

The Young Readers' Edition

PROLOGUE

March 1944

Our last Passover Seder together as a family is stamped into my memory forever. We were seated around a beautifully set table—my grandfather and grandmother, my father and mother, my uncle Eugene and aunt Irene, and my two younger siblings, Eugene and Alfred. Baby Judit was in her crib. The candles burned in their candlesticks, the fine dishes were laid out, and the heads of the family—my grandfather, my father, and my uncle—were leaning on cushions to symbolize relaxation and freedom from slavery in Egypt. After the reading and singing of the Passover story, we had a dinner of several courses that lasted about four hours.

I glanced around the table, thinking about all the troubles we had faced in the last years while this terrible war raged around the world. I hoped that my father and

Uncle Eugene would soon be permanently released from their labour battalion far from our home in the country once called Czechoslovakia. I hoped that we would soon have more food and clothing, just as we'd had before the war began. I hoped that I would no longer have to wear the Star of David on every article of my clothing: the badge that made me and other Jews feel like second-class citizens, made us feel as if we didn't belong.

We weren't aware then that many Jews in other countries had it so much worse than we did. We didn't know that Jews were being tortured and killed in terrible prisons called concentration camps. We hoped that the Russian Red Army would soon free us from the rules and laws that restricted our own freedom—rules that had been put in place by the evil Adolf Hitler. We hoped the war would end soon.

We had no idea that something terrible was coming. We were here together and celebrating on this special night. When the meal ended and everything was cleared away, we washed the dishes and prepared the table for the second Seder the following night. Around midnight, we went out into our yard to get some air before finally going to bed.

At 2:00 a.m., we were awoken to the sound of someone knocking at our gate. Farkas, my loyal Alsatian dog, began barking furiously as if he sensed there was trouble. We all got up and gathered together. Father opened a window and leaned outside to see who was there at this early hour.

"I need to speak to you right away!" a man called out to my father. He wanted to get through the gate so he could enter the property with his horse and wagon. The visitor turned out to be a man we knew well. Father opened the gate, and the man sped in. "I've just come from the pub," he said, breathlessly. "I overheard several police say that they were planning to round up all the Jews from town and remove them from their homes. I have no idea where they'll take you. But it's not good."

What does this mean? I looked at my father and grandfather, pale in the dim light. My mother wrapped a protective arm around my two brothers.

"I'm here to help you," the man continued. "You must come with me in my wagon. I'll drive you to the forest and find you a safe place to hide until the danger passes." Then he added, "Please, we don't have much time."

My father, grandfather, and uncle huddled in a corner, heads together while I watched and waited. Finally, they turned to face the visitor.

"Thank you for the offer, but we can't come with you," my grandfather said firmly. "It's Passover, and it's the Sabbath. It's impossible for us to travel on this important holy day."

The man's face fell, and he hung his head. "Please reconsider! I think you are all in danger."

Father shook his head. "It's hard to imagine something so terrible is about to happen," he said. Then he thanked the man and led him to the door.

As I lay back in bed, my mind was spinning, reliving the man's warning over and over. *What if the man is right?* I wondered. *Should we have listened to him? Should we have left?* But there was nothing I could do. Father and grandfather were the decision-makers in my family. We had to listen to them.

I had no idea that this decision would change our lives forever.

1

"How do you know which mushrooms I can eat?"

I was called Tibor when I was a child. I was born in 1929 in Moldava nad Bodvou, a town in the eastern part of the country that was then called Czechoslovakia. Our town had approximately five thousand people in it, mostly Christians. There were ninety Jewish families, mine among them. I grew up on a large farm with space for several of my family members. My grandfather, Raphael, and grandmother, Malvina, lived in one area of the home; my uncle Eugene and aunt Irene in another. And I lived with my mother, father, and siblings in the third. Ours was a sprawling compound with fruit orchards, plenty of land, and grain-fed chickens and ducks that roamed everywhere.

My younger brother Eugene (left), Alfred, and me in 1939.

My grandfather and Uncle Eugene operated a lumber business on our property. I loved all my family members, but I was especially close to my grandfather. He had fought on the Russian front in the First World War, years before I was born. And he'd been a cavalry officer in the Austro-Hungarian Empire, which had been formed in 1867 with Franz Joseph as emperor. Our family admired the emperor greatly, and my grandfather fought proudly in his army. He even had his old officer's cavalry uniform up in the attic, along with all the medals he had been awarded. My grandfather was strong and smart. I loved working side by side with him in the lumberyard, even when I had to shovel the manure left by the horses that came into our compound pulling the wagons where orders of lumber were piled.

"No matter what job you have to do," my grandfather always said as he worked next to me, sweeping horse manure, "make sure you do the job well."

Sometimes, my grandfather invited me to come with him when he went to buy sections of nearby forests to add to our supply of lumber. One day, I walked with him through a small grove of pine trees, pausing to smell the scent of pine and hear the wind blowing through the branches. My grandfather stopped next to a tall tree, checking its height and width. I knew he was looking for the perfect trees to cut down. I glanced around, feeling the thickness of the forest closing in.

"How do you know how to get out of here?" I asked. There was no obvious path in or out of the pine grove, and every direction looked the same to me.

My grandfather smiled. "There are signs everywhere," he said, pointing to the position of the sun in the sky and the shadows that had been cast by the trees behind us. "You just have to know where to look for them."

Then he pointed to the ground below us. "Your mother and grandmother would love to add those mushrooms to our dinner." He bent to pluck several white mushrooms from the soft earth. "Tibor, do you know how to tell a poisonous mushroom from one that we can eat?"

I shook my head and came closer, knowing that my grandfather was about to teach me a lesson.

"If the gills are brown like these are," he said, turning the mushroom over and pointing to the dark area under the cap and surrounding the stem, "then the mushroom is probably a good one."

"Probably," I repeated, nodding my head. I learned so many skills from my grandfather just by watching and listening to him.

After working with my grandfather in the lumber-yard, I often went to see my father at the pub he owned, which was called the Cellar. He had opened the Cellar years before I was born, and people came from all over to drink and socialize. A popular beverage was liqueur, a flavoured and sweetened alcoholic drink. Sometimes, after school let out and on the way to the Cellar, I stopped at a bakery in town to pick up some soft, yeasty buns. My father would let me open the cork on a barrel of liqueur and dip my bun into the sweet mixture. All my friends wanted to come with me on those days!

My father filled empty bottles with liqueur from casks that he kept. I had an important job putting fancy labels on the bottles of liqueur. I also put red wax on the corks and added my father's seal to the wax. The bottles looked as if they had never been opened. Then, I placed each bottle into a woven sleeve that was dusted with white chalk powder. That made the bottle look older than it was. There were times when my father let me deliver bottles of liqueur to customers in town.

I took the responsibility of all my jobs at the Cellar very seriously. My father was strict and demanded that I work hard and do a good job. I was never sure I measured up to his expectations of me. But I knew I didn't want to disappoint him.

2

"Eugene was the smart one

in the family."

I often waited at the Cellar for my father to close up so we could walk home together. A tall fence enclosed our compound. It had a main gate for cars, trucks, and wagons and a separate small gate to walk through. Farkas was the first one to greet me as I came through the gate. I always felt safe and well protected by our large white Alsatian that stood guard on our property. He had a bark that would scare off any unwanted visitors. We had two other dogs, fox terriers named Ali and Prince, but there was no question that Farkas was the one in charge.

I passed an old, rusted convertible that sat in a corner of our front yard, buried in the mud down to its axles. My father had driven the car for years until it finally broke down and couldn't be repaired. Some people might have thought of it as a piece of junk. But I loved sitting in the rusted car and pretending to drive. I passed by the chickens and ducks and heard the geese in their separate enclosure, where they were fed boiled corn to fatten them up. Then I entered our home and was greeted by the aroma of my mother's cooking. My father may have been the provider in our family, but my mother was the one in charge of our home. She cooked every day, feeding my siblings and me nutritious meals from scratch. She was a gifted seamstress and made many of our clothes. Once a year, she picked plums from our orchard and, along with other family members, made dozens of jars of black plum jam. She did crafts for our synagogue and helped the poor. She even learned how to knit dresses for herself. She had some help in the house from Anna, the Christian woman who had come to live with us when I was born. Anna was as much a part of my family as my blood relatives. But my mother was the one who ran the household. We had no running water in our home and no washing machine or other comforts. My mother never complained about any of this, and to this day, I don't know how she managed it all.

The other important member of my family was my aunt Bella. She loved to read, and I loved to read with her. At a young age, I would climb onto her lap and follow the stories in the books that she read aloud to me. That's where I learned to read Hungarian, and by the age of five, I was reading books on my own.

Aunt Bella had contracted polio as a child, a terrible disease that infected her spinal cord and meant that she couldn't move easily. Grandfather had to help her out of bed every morning, and Grandmother washed and dressed her. Then, Grandmother combed Bella's long, silky hair, braided it, and put it up in a bun on the top of her head. Despite her limitations, Aunt Bella was always happy and directed the activities in our home from her chair.

My brothers and I competed for Aunt Bella's attention. There was already a natural sibling rivalry between me and Eugene, who was three years younger than I was. Alfred, who was seven years younger than I, was lovable with his blond hair and blue eyes. Everyone, including me, spoiled him, and he was considered the baby of the family until Judit came along seven years after him. We all sat at Aunt Bella's feet, listening to her tell stories and begging for more.

Mother smiled at me when I entered the house at the end of a long day. "How was your day, Tibor?" she asked as she stirred a pot of meat stew that was bubbling on the stove. "Do you have homework?"

I nodded and moved over to the table, where Eugene was already bent over his books. Everyone thought of him as the smart one in the family. He could finish his homework with no problem and in record time. Aside from my love of books, I struggled with my studies, especially mathematics and grammar.

I went to two different schools. One was a regular public school, where I learned subjects like mathematics, geography, history, and art. Even though my family spoke Hungarian at home, at school we had to study Slovak, the official language of my country. The other school I attended was a Hebrew school, where I studied sacred Hebrew writings from the Bible and also learned Yiddish, the language spoken by many Jews.

One of the earliest memories I have is riding on the crossbar of my father's bicycle as he took me to Hebrew school for the very first time and introduced me to my teacher. I was only five years old then and terrified of this new place and of the teacher, with his grim face and the stick in one hand that he tapped against the palm of the other. I quickly learned that he wasn't afraid to use that stick if I didn't learn the text properly. And the more he punished me, the less I wanted to learn.

Reading was the one thing that saved me. And the books I loved most were those with cowboys and bandits. Those books were filled with adventure and danger and great suspense. One time, my friend Gaby Lichtman and I ran from Hebrew school to his house to get some books to read before evening prayers. Every day at Hebrew school, we would stop at sundown to pray in the synagogue, then return to school until 7:00 p.m. It was wintertime and we knew we only had ten minutes to grab some books and be back at synagogue before the sunset. I quickly stuffed several under my shirt and winter coat. But we were late, and by the time we got to the synagogue, the services had already started. I got into line with the rest of the students and said my prayers, keeping my head down and trying to be invisible. It didn't work. The teacher saw me and walked over, his face dark with anger. I knew I was in trouble. It was one thing to be punished for bad behaviour in class in front of my friends and classmates. But I didn't want to be punished here in front of the entire synagogue congregation, including my father, who was also there for prayers. My teacher raised his arm to slap me across the face and I twisted away. That's when all the books I had been hiding under my shirt came tumbling out and onto the synagogue floor.

My face burned with shame, and I wanted the floor to swallow me up, especially when I saw the look of disappointment on my father's face. I had seen that look before. And now, not only would I be punished by my father when I got home, but I knew that all the books I wanted to read—all those stories of adventure that I loved so much—would be taken away from me.

The only thing I hoped was that my mother would come to my rescue, as she often did. Her understanding was what I counted on.

3

"The first time I heard Hitler speak."

t was one day in 1938 when ten of my father's friends came to our home to listen to a speech by Adolf Hitler on my father's radio. Hitler spoke in German, but I knew enough of the language to make out his threatening message.

"We are going to eradicate all the Jews of Europe!" he ranted.

My stomach dropped as I glanced around the room. The shocked looks on the faces of my father and his friends did little to ease my fears. I was only nine years old, but I felt something terrible was going to happen.

I knew that Hitler was evil and unpredictable, and he and his Nazi Party hated Jews. In his desire for land and power, he had threatened to wage war in Europe unless an area of Czechoslovakia in the west known as Sudetenland was handed over to him. The leaders of Britain and France held a conference in Munich, Germany, in September 1938 to talk about this situation. Those countries believed that if they gave Sudetenland over to Hitler, he would be satisfied. In exchange for his promise of peace, Sudetenland was turned over to him in an agreement known as the Munich Agreement. Our president, Edvard Beneš, wasn't even present for that conference and had no say in what was going to happen.

It was no surprise that Hitler did not keep his end of the bargain.

He wanted more land and more power. In October 1938, President Beneš resigned and went into exile in England. Hitler defied the Munich Agreement and marched into Czechoslovakia, occupying the whole country. Czechoslovakia, as I had known it growing up, no longer existed. We were divided into three regions, and my area in the eastern part of the country was given to Hungary, under the leadership of the dictator Regent Miklós Horthy.

There was a parade scheduled on the day the Hungarian authorities marched into my town. The red, white, and green flag of Hungary hung from shops and homes, surrounded by ribbons of the same colours. In school, we learned to sing the Hungarian national anthem to greet the new rulers when they arrived. There was a sign at the entrance of town that read

Welcome our Hungarian liberators!

On the day of the parade, my grandfather took me up to the attic, where he stored his cavalry uniform from the days of the Austro-Hungarian Empire. We cleaned his clothes, brushed and polished his boots, and attached all his medals. When he had dressed in his uniform, I stood back and looked at him in awe.

"How do I look, Tibor?" he asked, pulling back his shoulders and thrusting out his chest.

"Wonderful!" I was breathless in front of his impressive stature.

Grandfather joined all the other Jewish veterans at the welcoming gate to greet the Hungarian troops. All the townspeople were there. A few hours later, I saw a column of soldiers approaching, led by an officer on horseback, slowly marching closer. These soldiers did not impress me. Compared to my grandfather in his polished outfit, they had dirty uniforms full of patches.

A cheer went up from the crowd, and everyone sang the Hungarian anthem as the military column marched into the town square. The welcoming committee handed over our town to the new Hungarian administration. The ceremony ended, and the soldiers were dismissed and allowed to wander throughout the town. They headed to the pubs, where townspeople gave them food. My father's pub, the Cellar, had a big sign outside that read

Free drinks to our liberators!

Within two days, my father's entire supply of alcohol was gone.

I didn't fully understand at the time what this change in government would mean for the Jews of my town. My parents and other family members hid their fears from me. But even though my grandfather dressed in his military finery and my father doled out food and alcohol with other pub owners, I could sense, from hushed conversations and sombre faces, that my family and all the other Jewish families were afraid of the future. We knew that Regent Horthy was a friend of Hitler and Nazi Germany. We knew that, like Hitler, he hated Jews and would do whatever he could to make our lives difficult. We had to find ways to play up to the new government and demonstrate our support—show them that we were not a threat. But we didn't know if this would work.

Within a few days, I had my first encounter with a Hungarian soldier who hated Jews. I was crossing into town over the railway tracks and was stopped by a Hungarian guard who recognized that my cap was Jewish. He yelled out, "You dirty Jew, where are you going?" I stopped in my tracks as he approached me, fear prickling across my skin. He pointed at my cap. "You should take that off when you see me. Show some respect." I quickly removed my cap and, luckily, he allowed me to pass. When I told my father what had happened, he prepared small bottles of alcohol for me to carry on the streets.

"Offer any guards a sample of this," he said, grim-faced. "It should allow you to get past anyone who tries to harass you."

The bribe worked, and I managed to walk in the streets without being hassled. But within a short time, there were more and more incidents where Jews like me were singled out for discrimination. People shouted ugly, hurtful names in my direction. Kids who had previously ignored me picked fights with me and my Jewish friends. The newspapers were filled with cartoons that showed Jews with hooked noses, wearing dirty clothing. Articles appeared suggesting that Jews would flood into town in hordes and endanger the lives of the locals. This kind of propaganda was everywhere, intended to mislead the public into thinking that Jews were evil and dangerous. Of course, these were all lies. But I began to realize that this propaganda—these lies, repeated often enough—would eventually be believed by many who were hearing them. These lies would be seen as the truth. I hated the lies and was ashamed that people saw me and other Jews in this hateful, hurtful way.

Meanwhile, I knew that the Jewish community of my town had to stay hopeful that, with time, the discrimination would pass. It was still only 1939, and we had many unknown and unthinkable obstacles ahead of us. My family was still together, and we prayed that things would soon return to normal.

4

"I heard Farkas barking ferociously."

Nothing returned to normal. Things only got worse. By 1940, we could no longer own radios, and all Jews had to turn over their sets to the new government. Without our radios, there was no way we might be warned about any potential dangers. All Jewish families had to be photographed by the police. We had weekly cadet drills at school with a military officer. Non-Jewish students marched at the front of the columns and carried wooden guns, while Jewish students were always ordered to the back of the line and made to carry rakes and shovels. When we arrived at the shooting range, we had to rake and clean the area while the others practised drills. I hated being made to feel inferior next to my classmates.

My whole body shook with shame during these weekly drills.

Another law was passed stating that Jewish families could no longer employ non-Jews. That meant that Anna, our beloved housekeeper, could not be with us anymore.

"I won't go," she said angrily, crossing her arms in front of her. "They can't make me."

But of course, they could. Within days of that law, the police arrived on our doorstep and escorted Anna from our home. My mother hugged her tightly before she left, while I stood by watching and worrying. The hope that things would soon return to normal was fading faster and faster.

When a law was passed saying that Jews could no longer sell alcohol, we knew my father's business was in trouble. Soon, he was forced to turn over the key to the Cellar to the authorities. But even that was not the worst of it. In 1941, all Jewish males from eighteen to forty-five were sent away to work in mines, forests, and military installations on the Eastern Front. My father and uncle packed winter clothing and said goodbye to the rest of us.

"When will we see you again?" my mother asked, her eyes sunken and hollow.

"They say we'll be allowed to come home for one week in the year," my father replied, looking away.

After that, it was up to my mother to meet all the demands of the household. My siblings and I tried to help wherever we could. Other members of our Jewish community distributed supplies where needed. It was especially painful on the Jewish High Holidays when I looked around the synagogue and realized that there were only women, children, and old people left to attend the services.

In August 1942, a few of my friends came to our orchard to pick fruit for their families. I was already thirteen years old, and as we stuffed ourselves with plums, we challenged each other to see who could climb highest in a very tall walnut tree. We knew it was dangerous because you could easily miss a branch and fall, injuring yourself badly. But for those few minutes playing in our orchard, we felt happy and free from worry.

Suddenly, I heard Farkas barking ferociously, warning us that strangers had entered our yard. Mother called for me to come back to the house. My friends disappeared, running to their homes. When I got inside, two police officers were reading a document to my family members. I had no idea what was in it, but from the sombre looks on the faces of my grandparents, my mother, and my aunts, I knew it had to be serious.

I soon discovered that it was an order that my mother, Aunt Irene, my siblings, and I each pack a small bundle and prepare to leave our home. My grandparents, along with Aunt Bella, were not included in this directive. They could stay.

"But where are you taking us?" my mother asked. The police officer shook his head and didn't answer.

My grandfather pleaded with him. "You can't do this! Our family has lived in this area for generations. We're citizens."

"We're following orders," the police officer replied grimly. "There's nothing you can do about it."

We ran through the house grabbing clothes and food and stuffed the items into individual backpacks. Just before we left, my grandfather came up to my mother.

"Here," he whispered, placing some money into her hands. The police had their backs to us and didn't see the exchange. "You never know when you might need this."

Mother slipped the money into her pack and continued grabbing supplies. Finally, we placed the bundles on our backs and the police escorted us out of our home. Farkas howled loudly and had to be held back by my grandfather. His barks and cries rang in my ears.

We were taken to a train station and, along with about eighty other people, loaded onto an open cattle car. We had no idea where we were going and no idea how long we'd be forced to stand like this. The train pulled out of the station. Everyone looked tense and uncertain. Mother and Aunt Irene tried as best they could to keep us together in one spot, but it wasn't easy as we bumped and butted against each other, trying to adjust to the movement of the train under our feet. At one point, my mother slipped the money that Grandfather had given her into my hands.

"Hide this somewhere, Tibor," she whispered. "I'm afraid I may lose my backpack." Mother stumbled as the train swerved around a corner. I reached out a hand to steady her and tightened my grip on the money. No one paid much attention to me as I slipped it into the lining of my boots.

Our first stop was the city of Kassa, about sixty kilometres away. That was where our cattle car was attached to other cars already loaded with people. From there, we continued on, eventually arriving at a station in the region of Transylvania. Shortly after our arrival, several Jewish men and women from the area showed up to hand out fruit, bread, and water. It was a relief to fill our stomachs, and we were grateful for the food. But we were not allowed off the train and had to remain standing upright for the entire night. To make it worse, we had to use two buckets for toilets. The smell was foul and overwhelming. And as the night wore on, my body shook with fear, made worse by the cold night air. Older people around me groaned and cried out, "When will we go home? When will we be free?" No one answered their cries.

We stayed on the train for nearly six days, passing town after town, going first in one direction, and then turning and going back in the opposite direction. We couldn't understand where our captors were taking us. The fear and lack of sleep began to wear at our bodies and our minds. Just when we thought we couldn't take it anymore, we pulled into a small station and were ordered to gather our belongings and leave the train. We joined about a thousand people from the other cattle cars, and we all assembled on the platform. Military police surrounded us and began to push and prod us up a steep, rocky road until we reached a mountain plateau that had several large sheds. The police shoved us into lines in front of long tables that had been set up. I stood next to my family members, slowly trudging forward and watching as other families approached the police seated behind those tables. The officers asked for identification and demanded to search the bundles that people had brought.

"Hand over your valuables," the police shouted. "Anyone caught hiding anything will be punished."

People began to pull out jewellery, money, gold coins, and other treasures, which they placed on the table in front of the guards. I watched as one family approached and laid jars of preserves on the table.

"That's all we've brought," the father of the family declared. "There's nothing here of value."

The police officer did not believe him and opened one of the jars of jam. He dipped his finger into the jar and pulled out a gold watch and several rings on a chain. Strawberry jam dripped from the jewellery that the officer held up in front of him. That family was beaten for hiding the items.

"Mother," I whispered urgently, "I've got the money you gave me inside my boot." It suddenly felt like a boulder under my foot. "I'm afraid I'm going to be caught."

The colour drained from my mother's face. "Just try to act normally," she said as we approached the table.

"Documents," the officer said. My mother placed our identification papers in front of him. He examined them closely. I tried to keep my face as blank as possible while my foot throbbed.

Finally, the officer looked up. "Where are the men in your family?"

"They've been sent to work in labour battalions," my mother replied. I marvelled at how even and calm her voice was.

The officer paused for one more minute as his eyes scanned the faces of my family. I could almost hear my heart pounding in my ears. Finally, he said, "Move on!"

Mother gathered our documents and we walked past him. I breathed a deep sigh of relief.

5

- - - - - -

"Families who went before us

had written their names on

the wall of the shed."

We were marched to a shed, where we bedded down with about three hundred people on a sawdust floor. The sawdust was much more comfortable than the open trains that had brought us here. But the shed was hot during the day and cold and drafty at night. We staked out a spot for our family, and this became our home for the next two weeks.

We fetched drinking water from quite a distance away, guarded all the time by soldiers. There was never enough water to bathe or wash our clothes. The only food we received was one bowl of soup each day. But the money I had hidden in my boot became a blessing. We used it to buy a small loaf of black rye bread from locals who came to the place where we filled our water pails. Exchanging money for bread was dangerous, and we could only do it when the soldiers who guarded us were out of sight. We paid a huge amount for that bread, much more than it would have cost at any bakery. But what choice did we have? In the weeks that we were there, the bread nourished us, and we shared it with others who were also hungry.

At the end of the second week, a Hungarian officer appeared and ordered all of us to line up outside our shed.

"Tomorrow, you will be taken in trucks to your workplace," he shouted. He had a moustache and rode a big horse. "Pack your bundles and be outside early in the morning."

The walls of our shed were covered with the names of families who had come before us. People we never knew had written their names on the wooden planks, along with the day of their departure and the name of their destination. There must have been thousands of names from previous transports scribbled on the wall, each one a life marker, a record to remind the world that these people had once been here.

We wrote our names on the wall of the shed, just as the others before us had done. The next morning, we were loaded onto trucks and the officer wished us a good journey. The trucks climbed high into the hills above the sheds and then descended on the other side. All of a sudden, we heard some yelling. I turned around to see the officer with the moustache galloping toward us at full speed.

"Stop the truck!" he shouted.

The truck ground to a halt, throwing all of us against one another. My stomach tightened, wondering what this was all about.

"You are not going to the workplace," the officer announced when he had caught up. "Instead, you will be going home."

Had I heard him correctly? It took a moment for the announcement to sink in. I glanced at my family members, who looked as stunned as I felt. Suddenly, we all started to cheer, along with the others in our truck. All I could think about was my home, my grandparents, my dogs, and getting back to a normal life.

"Get off the trucks, now," the officer continued. "You can walk down to the train station. You'll have to buy your own tickets for the journey home. Those who have money can pay for those who don't." And with that, he galloped off again.

Still stunned, we got off the trucks and walked down the hill to the waiting train. Hundreds of us filled the entire train. This time, we were not in cattle cars. We sat in seats like normal people. We were a dirty, smelly bunch, but we were happy to be going home.

When the train stopped in our town a few days later, we gathered our belongings, got off, and started to walk toward our home. As we came around a bend in the road, I could see our house, the most beautiful sight. As we got closer, Farkas came flying through the gate at full speed. He jumped up on me, licking me all over my face.

My grandparents were waiting for us in the yard and had tears in their eyes as they hugged us. I had an emotional reunion with Aunt Bella, and then my grandmother began to prepare a feast to welcome us back. The table practically sagged under the weight of the chicken, salads, and other goodies she made. I couldn't eat fast enough!

After the meal, I ran outside to check on the chickens, ducks, and geese in the yard. The orchard was bursting with ripening fruit. I hugged every single tree. This was one of the happiest moments of my life. Things got even better when my father and uncle arrived home several days later. They had managed to get away from their labour battalion and came looking for us, travelling from station to station and asking if anyone had seen a transport of Jewish people in cattle cars. They eventually tracked us back to our home, and we were happily reunited. We were a complete family once again.

I never learned why we had been suddenly released and sent home. What I did learn, many years later, was that our group was the only one that had survived that deportation. Forty thousand Jewish people had gone before us, and all were killed by mobile units known as Nazi Einsatzgruppen. This was the first mass murder of Jews by the Nazis in the Second World War.

All those people who had written their names on the wall of our shed and other sheds were gone.

6

- - - - -

"You have five minutes to pack your things."

By now, so many more laws and rules had been introduced to restrict our freedom. All the Jewish students in my school had to sit at the back of the classroom. We all felt humiliated and singled out by the other students and the teachers. Food and material for clothing were severely limited for all Jews. All Jewish people were ordered to wear the yellow six-pointed Star of David on every article of clothing we owned. That star was an important symbol of my faith. But now, I felt ashamed to have to wear it wherever I went. It made me feel like an outsider, someone who didn't belong. Of course, we had no choice about these laws and no power to refuse to obey them. All I could hope was that maybe, just maybe, these would be the last laws. That was not to be.

It was March 1944, and we were about to celebrate Passover, the important Jewish holiday that commemorates the time in Egypt when Jews were freed from slavery. My family was seated around a beautifully set table—my grandfather and grandmother, my father and mother, Uncle Eugene and Aunt Irene, my siblings Eugene and Alfred. Baby Judit was in her crib. Judit had been born the previous December, a beautiful girl with brown hair and dark eyes. At first, I wasn't sure how I felt about this baby girl who was so much younger than I. I wondered how we would take care of another addition to the family. Besides, with all the laws and rules in place, this was not a good time for a Jewish child to be born.

The only person missing from our table was my aunt Bella. She had died the previous year, and her death left a huge hole in my life and in the lives of my family members. I missed spending time with her. I missed the stories she read to me and my siblings. In retrospect, maybe her death was a bit of a blessing. She would not have to suffer through what was to come for the rest of us. At that time, we weren't aware that many Jews in other countries were being tortured and killed in concentration camps. We hoped the war would end soon. We hoped the rules and restrictions would disappear. We had no idea that something terrible was coming. We were here together and celebrating on this special night.

We went to bed after midnight and were awoken around 2:00 a.m. by a man pounding at our gate. He rushed in to warn us that he had overheard someone at the pub say that the police would be rounding up Jews.

"I have no idea where they will take you," he said.

He urged my family to come with him in his wagon and said he'd find a safe place for us to hide. But my grandfather said no. He reminded the man that it was Passover and the Sabbath.

"It's impossible for us to travel on this important holy day," my grandfather said firmly.

Disappointed, the man left, and I went back to bed, troubled by his dire warning.

I fell into a fitful sleep that lasted only a few hours before there was pounding at the gates once more. This time, they were forced open. Two police officers barged into our home.

"You have five minutes to pack your things before we take you away!" one of them shouted. "Hand over your money and valuables. You won't need those things where you're going."

I was in a daze, the visitor's warning still playing through my mind like a broken record. My mother grabbed my baby sister, Judit, and held her close.

"Put on layers of clothing," she whispered urgently to me and my brothers. "We don't know how long we'll be away."

"And don't forget your winter boots," father added.

Mother began packing food into backpacks, murmuring under her breath about what she should take to feed the whole family.

"Hurry up," the police officers shouted. "You're being too slow." They prodded us with their rifles and rummaged through our dresser drawers, looking for anything they could steal.

My heart pounded and my mouth went dry. *We should have listened to the visitor*, I thought. *We should have heeded his warning*. Now it was too late.

As I layered my body with shirts, sweaters, pants, and jackets, our neighbour Illy rushed into our home. She was a Christian woman who had always been a good friend of ours.

"Get out!" the police yelled at Illy. "You have no business here."

She ignored them and turned to my mother. "Ethel, where are you taking the baby? Why don't you leave her with me? She'll be safer." She reached her arms out to take Judit.

Mother stiffened, pulled back, and shook her head, tightening her grip on my baby sister. "We have to stay together as a family," my mother whispered.

Illy's arms fell to her sides. To this day, I wonder what would have become of Judit had my mother accepted Illy's offer. That is something I will never know.

At that moment, the police stepped in again. They pushed us all out the door—my grandmother and grandfather, my uncle Eugene and aunt Irene, my mother and father, my two brothers, Judit, and me. Hours earlier we had been enjoying our Passover Seder, retelling the story of Jews being freed from slavery in Egypt. And now, we were being forced to leave our home.

We struggled to carry our bundles, and my grandmother could hardly lift hers. As I left, I said a silent and sad goodbye to my home, to the orchard, and to Farkas. My gut told me that this deportation would be so much more serious than the one in 1942. This time, my whole family was being taken away. Who would take care of our home while we were gone, and when would I see it again?

7

- - - - - -

"Townspeople yelled and cursed us as we passed."

arkas barked and howled furiously behind me as my entire family, along with about four hundred other Jews from my town, were led through the streets, guarded by soldiers on all sides, as if we were criminals being taken to jail. We walked past neighbours and other townspeople, some of whom sneered and jeered at us, calling us horrible names and spitting at us as we passed.

How can they do this? I wondered. *Why have they turned on us?*

We had lived next to one another my whole life. Many of these people had shopped in our Jewish stores, had bought lumber from my grandfather, and had come to my father's tavern before it was forced to close down. So many of these townspeople had bought goods on credit from Jews like my grandfather. Perhaps they were happy they wouldn't have to pay the money back. There were even kids my age who stared out at us from behind their curtained windows. I lowered my head so no one would see the anger and shame that burned on my face.

We arrived at the public school in the centre of town, where we were divided into two groups and crammed into two rooms. That night was so hard for all of us. People gathered in whispered conversations. *Where do you think we're going? When are we going to come back? What will become of us?* No one could answer those questions. Some people tried to sleep, but there were babies crying non-stop. There were some pails of water for washing, but only one outhouse for all of us to use. There was no room to move, and I could feel the fear from everyone around me.

Morning finally came, and we were ordered into the schoolyard with our bundles. From there, we were marched to the railway station, passing our own property along the way. I glanced across the orchard, thinking that I should have been waking up to a Passover breakfast with special coffee saved for this holiday and matzah—the thin Passover cracker—broken into little pieces and covered with hot milk and sugar. Instead, I was marching past my home with an empty stomach and no idea of what was ahead of me. To make it worse, I could see that someone had moved into our home overnight, taking over our property as if we had never been there. Farkas was barking as if he sensed that we were passing close by and was wailing goodbye to us. It felt as if he was the only one who seemed to care that we were being taken away.

At the station, we boarded the train to Kassa, the same city that had been our first stop when we were deported two years earlier. We were told we would be staying with Jewish families in one area of the city, and we ended up in the home of the doctor who had taken care of Aunt Bella before she died. His family lived in a three-bedroom apartment that now included the ten members of my family. Food was scarce, but we managed to find enough for all of us. We slept on mattresses on the floor, which had to be cleared away in the morning. We wondered how long we would have to stay here. Soon enough, we had our answer.

Within a week, notices were posted directing the Jewish families on several streets to gather their belongings and walk to a brickyard on the outskirts of the city. Those who were listed on the notices had to be there on the designated day or suffer harsh punishment. Each day after that, we checked to see which streets were to be moved out. When we didn't see our street name, we always felt a bit of relief. At the same time, we were also extremely tense. We knew our time would come, and we had to be prepared. We needed supplies for whatever journey was ahead of us, but we had to think carefully about what we would take with us and how much. The walk to the brickyard was two kilometres and we knew it would be difficult to carry too much, especially for my grandparents and for my mother, who also carried baby Judit.

My heart sank the day they posted the order for our street to go. We said goodbye to another place that had sheltered us and walked outside, where the streets were filled with Jewish people, young and old, struggling with their loads—all headed in the same direction. It took us several hours to reach the brickyard. We were taken to a large shed that was used for drying bricks. Red dust covered the rough floor. Hundreds of people scrambled for a place to sit. We staked out an area, and my father, my uncle, and I went outside to look around.

"That smell!" I gagged and covered my nose as my uncle pointed at the only outdoor toilet for the thousands of people that were there.

"And look over there," my father said, indicating the barbed wire that surrounded the entire brickyard and the guards who patrolled. "We're prisoners in here."

We had no choice but to try to adjust to this terrible place. The worst for me was the constant hunger. We were fed only one bowl of soup each day. We quickly finished off the supplies we had brought with us. I learned that I could get one slice of bread if I volunteered with other teens to clean up former Jewish areas in the city that would now be occupied by non-Jewish families. I went to the main gate nearly every day, hoping I'd be chosen for this work detail and opportunity for a piece of bread.

We stayed in the brickyard for three weeks. Every day at noon, an officer from the SS—Nazi elite troops—would arrive, and we would all gather to hear what he had to say.

"You will all be resettled in the east," he told us. "Your families will stay together, and you will be working on farms."

The officer came back every day for days to repeat this message. I started to believe him—we all did! A farm in the east didn't sound so bad, especially after this terrible place. Maybe we'd even see some of my mother's relatives who had been deported a couple of years earlier. They had written postcards to us saying that they were all together and eagerly waiting for us to arrive. It would be wonderful to meet up with my cousins and extended family. I couldn't wait to leave this place. Anything sounded better than where we were. But it was all a terrible lie, though I couldn't have understood that at the time. We were about to be put on trains and taken to a place that was far worse than the terrible brickyard. Just like all the propaganda that had come before, this lie and the promise of work in the east, repeated every day for days, was designed to get us on those trains willingly and peacefully.

8

"Raus, *get out fast!*"

After three weeks in the brickyard, we were ordered to get ready to be transported. We packed up our small bundles and made our way to the loading area at the station, where the cattle cars were waiting. Each train car was given one pail of drinking water and an empty pail to use as a toilet. One hundred of us, along with our small bundles, were crammed into each car, and then the doors were locked. This did not feel like the last time we had been transported away and later sent home. This time, additional members of my family were on the transport—my grandfather, my grandmother, who was frail, and my nine-month-old sister, Judit. My gut told me that we were all in danger. What was happening to us and where were we going to end up?

We were stuck together in the cattle car, standing room only, and could hardly breathe properly in the heat. There was a small opening with bars near the ceiling for air. The water was gone almost immediately, and the toilet pail was never emptied. People moaned and cried out in pain. It unsettled me to be squeezed and surrounded by so many people. And I could only imagine how frightened my younger brothers must have felt. I was fifteen years old at the time. But Eugene was only twelve, and Alfred only nine. I wanted to protect them and my parents, but I couldn't even get close to any family member.

There are some things I will never forget about the journey: the smell of smoke, the sound of the train as it built up steam to pull thirty to forty loaded cars, the clicking of the wheels as they hit the rails. On the first day, the train stopped to refuel.

People shouted through another small opening in the cattle car. "Please," they begged of the guards who paraded up and down the platform. "Give us some water!"

A guard stopped to look at us. "Throw us your valuables," he replied. "Then, we'll give you water."

Some people threw pieces of hidden jewellery through the opening. Once the soldiers got the valuables, they simply laughed and walked away.

That first night, I fell asleep standing up, lulled by the rhythm of the train. I woke suddenly to the sound of the train's loud whistle. I thought I'd had a nightmare, but in reality, I was living the nightmare.

A cattle car at Auschwitz II–Birkenau.

After three days of travel, the train stopped, and I heard the doors of the other cattle cars being opened. I couldn't wait for ours to open as well. Finally, someone lifted the latch. Bright, harsh light flooded into our cattle car as the door slid open. A man wearing a striped cap, jacket, and pants yelled, *"Raus, schnell!"* From the little German I knew, I understood this to mean "get out fast!"

I thought the man who wore this kind of striped uniform must be a criminal. Did he think *we* were criminals? This had to be a mistake.

"*Raus, schnell,*" he shouted again and again.

I wanted to move, but I couldn't. And when I was finally pulled from the cattle car, my legs could hardly hold me up. All the people were hauled out, including my mother with my baby sister still in her arms, my father, my grandparents, and my uncle and aunt. We were all numb from the journey and confused by the lights and harsh orders that were being barked at us. On top of that, the smell of smoke nearly overwhelmed me. I had no idea what that was.

There were more men in striped clothing on the platform, along with SS soldiers and officers dressed in sharp and shiny uniforms. They ordered us into two lines: men on one side and women on the other. Older men and children joined the women's line. I stood next to my father and my uncle.

I glanced over at my grandparents, my aunt, my mother, and my siblings in the other group. Both groups were marched away. Everything happened so fast. I had no chance to say goodbye.

9

"Keep an eye on your boots."

I was dazed, still trying to understand where I was and what was happening.

Still struggling with the disappearance of my mother and other family members who had been taken away with no chance to talk.

Still wondering when I'd see them again.

There was no time to sort out any of this as my father, uncle, and I were moved on, first to a building where we were ordered to hand over any remaining documents and jewellery. Our hair was cut by more men in striped clothing. One of them wore a band on his arm that said "Kapo." That meant he was the boss. He checked to see if any of the prisoners had gold fillings in their teeth. If gold was found, that person was taken aside and the gold was removed with rusty pliers.

The next stage was the showers. I had never seen a shower before in my life, and I was in awe of the many shower heads and the large wheels that controlled the flow of the hot and cold water. Our clothes had already been taken from us. I was filled with a feeling of shame at being crammed together with other naked prisoners, mixed with the fear that had not left me since the moment I arrived. We were ordered to lay our boots on the edge of the shower while we washed. My father, uncle, and I kept a close eye on our boots because they were custom-made and practically new. We knew they would last for a long time. Suddenly, the Kapo and his helpers began to move through the shower area, collecting all the boots.

"Tibor," my father warned, nudging me toward the edge. "Get the boots before those men take them."

I scrambled over and grabbed our boots, and we kept them under our arms while we continued to shower. We didn't fully realize at the moment how important this quick action had been. Had we lost those boots, our lives would have been even more at risk. If your feet were not protected, you would not be able to work. And if you couldn't work, you would be killed. Those who lost their boots were lucky if they got a pair of wooden clogs instead. But these clogs were more like pieces of wood with canvas tops stapled to them, and they were

Auschwitz II–Birkenau, showing the train ramp, five crematoria with gas chambers, fire pit, and the arrival ramp.

The guardhouse and entrance to Auschwitz II–Birkenau.

damaging to the feet. Our boots were treasures that we had to guard day and night.

While we were washing, an SS guard stood beside one of the big wheels that controlled the water temperature. He suddenly turned it to scalding hot. As we tried to jump away to avoid getting burned, another guard with a bat in his hand began beating us to get back under the flow. Then the first guard turned the water freezing cold. I was just beginning to realize how cruel these SS guards could be. They could use us for their own entertainment whenever and however they wanted.

After the showers, we were marched to our barracks. Inside, there were rows of triple-tier bunks with no mattresses or blankets. The wooden planks were hard, but after three days of standing in the packed cattle car, it felt good to lie down. So much had happened in the few hours since our arrival, so much I couldn't understand or sort out. All I knew for certain was that I was scared about my future and what was in store for me. I was still so worried about my family, and worried about the guards who had already shown us their cruelty.

This was my introduction to the concentration camp called Auschwitz-Birkenau.

10

"Will we see our families today?"

"**R**aus, *schnell!*" That angry order and loud banging interrupted my short sleep. The Kapos ordered my father, uncle, and I, along with all the men in our barrack, outside. It was the first chance for me to look around in the daylight. This place was enormous—like a large industrial field. I later learned the camp was in occupied Poland and was the largest of the Nazi concentration camps. There were hundreds of barracks on either side of me. Thousands of thin and sick-looking people stood around me within the barbed-wire fences that enclosed us. Dozens of guard towers surrounded us, with SS soldiers inside manning machine guns and searchlights. Nearby, four huge chimneys belched angry red flames and smoke. The smell of smoke that had first overwhelmed me when I left the cattle car was everywhere, filling my nostrils and choking me.

"Pay attention, Tibor," my father whispered next to me. "If you hear the Kapos ordering you to do something, do it fast. Otherwise, they'll beat you."

I nodded as we were pushed forward to line up in single file in front of tables that were set up in front of our barracks. One by one, we were ordered to come forward and face two men who sat behind the table. I stood in line in between my father and uncle.

"Name!" the first man demanded when it was my turn to approach the table. He asked for my place and date of birth, what languages I spoke, my height and weight, and the colour of my hair. When I had answered his questions, he motioned me on to the second man, who tattooed a number on my left arm. I did my best not to flinch as the number was etched into my skin: A-9892. My father's number was A-9891 and my uncle's was A-9893. Wherever we went, I was always right between them. I believed they had become my guardian angels, protecting me on either side.

Nearby, there were piles of striped pants, jackets, and caps. I was handed one of each and put them on, but they didn't fit well. We had no socks or underwear, no belt or suspenders to hold up our pants. From a pile of rags, my father managed to find a pair of trousers, and with his teeth and fingers, he ripped off strips of material that he twisted into belts for the three of us. We stripped more pieces of cloth and wrapped them around our feet in place of socks. We also kept a small piece of cloth to use as toilet paper. My father and uncle seemed to know instinctively what we had to do in order to cope. We had already wisely kept our boots. They had figured out how we should dress from the rags that were offered to us. There would be many more situations to come in which they would teach me how to survive in these terrible conditions.

Once I put on these striped prisoner's clothes, I felt as if I were no longer a human being, only a number. Prisoner workers stamped a Star of David with my tattoo number on two strips of white material. They used a needle and thread to stitch one strip on the front left side of the striped jacket I wore and the other strip on the back. Different groups received different patches on their clothing to identify them. Political prisoners got a red triangle, Roma people a brown triangle, homosexuals a pink triangle, Jehovah's Witnesses a violet triangle, habitual criminals a green triangle, and so-called asocials whom the Nazis had deemed unfit for community life, like drug addicts or alcoholics, those people wore a black triangle. Of all the groups that were there, I knew that we Jews were the lowest and least valued group of all.

Soon, two prisoners arrived carrying a large canister of hot tea, my first food or drink in days. They gave us metal dishes, lined us up, and doled out the tea. It tasted quite different from what I was used to at home—thin and watery. It wasn't enough to fill my belly, which screamed out for food.

"Excuse me," my father asked as the men portioning out tea passed by. "Will we see our families today?"

"Where did you come from?" the man asked.

"We arrived from Hungary in the middle of the night," my father replied.

The man laughed. "It's 1944 and you don't know what this place is all about?" He pointed to one of the smoking chimneys. "That's where your families are."

My father's face was grim, and he turned away, realizing something that took me several more days to understand. When I finally made sense of the message, the weight of that knowledge crashed down on me like a sledgehammer. My family—mother, siblings, grandmother, grandfather, and aunt—had been sent to the gas chambers, cavernous buildings with shower heads like the ones in which we had had our first shower. But instead of water coming out of those shower heads, I learned that poisonous gas flowed from them, killing everyone inside. The bodies of those innocent Jews, including my family members, would then be burned in large ovens. That was the smoke that poured out of the tall chimneys, filling the sky and my nostrils.

My father and uncle never spoke of the deaths, and I tried not to think about them too much, either, knowing I would be overwhelmed by the horrible reality. It was only when I lay in my bunk at night that I felt the huge loss and allowed myself to grieve.

It was May 1944, and my family was gone.

11

-- -- -- -- --

"Should I eat the whole slice of bread?"

If there are farmers in the group, raise your hands!" An officer barked out the order to all the men who were lined up.

"Put up your hand, Tibor," my father whispered. "If we're put to work on a farm, we may be able to get some food—potatoes, turnips, or beets."

I was already so hungry and thirsty. I nodded and raised my hand along with my father and uncle. About a hundred of us were picked, and we were told we would be taken to another camp. I was already shocked by how my life was changing minute by minute and hour by hour. Everything about this place filled me with fear. How different would this new camp be from where we were?

The guards marched us several kilometres down the road to the camp that was called Auschwitz I. We passed under a large metal gate with the German words *Arbeit macht frei*. Work sets you free.

We were taken to a barrack where we were met by a Kapo who called himself Heinrich. He was a short man with piercing green eyes that seemed to look right through us. He had a green triangle on his jacket—most likely a murderer who had been released from a German jail and brought to the camp to be our work boss. He paced in front of us, holding a club in his hands.

"If you do not follow my orders," he bellowed, "your life will come to a speedy end. Tomorrow morning, you will have your first taste of Auschwitz I." I sensed immediately how dangerous he was.

We were not allowed to enter our barracks in this new camp until all the units had returned from work, and that meant we had a few hours to walk around and try to understand the layout of the camp. Barbed-wire fences enclosed the entire area. I could see a guardhouse close to the main gate with SS soldiers and attack dogs at the ready. Auschwitz I had more than two dozen two-storey red-brick buildings that would be our barracks, each one holding twelve hundred inmates. There was one washroom for each building. Near the main camp gate was a long kitchen building where prisoners prepared meals for approximately twenty-five thousand inmates and the SS guards. Several of the buildings were used as warehouses for the clothing and wool blankets that had been taken from those arriving by train. One barrack was used as a first-aid clinic where people with work-related injuries came for help. Barrack 21 housed a surgery, and the upper floors were used as hospital wards for patients. Next to barrack 21 was the building used for medical experiments on inmates.

When it was time for the other units to return to the camp, we rushed to the gate to watch them march inside in rows of five. The head of each unit reported the number of prisoners to a guard; this ensured that the same number of people who left in the morning also returned in the evening. It took over two hours for all the units to march back into camp. With the return of these prisoners, we were finally allowed to enter our barracks. I could see that we would be sleeping on the same triple-tiered bunk beds that we'd had previously. But now we had mattresses instead of just wooden slats. The mattresses had once been filled with straw, but after years of use by previous prisoners, they had become bags of dust. On top of each mattress sat a smelly, dirty blanket.

The men who had returned rushed to the washing stations to clean themselves and rinse out their jackets and pants. I was already learning how important it was to stay as clean as possible. If we didn't, lice could easily overwhelm our bodies and multiply, spreading typhus, a serious disease that could lead to death. The men wrung out their clothes and put them back on while still wet. Nobody had any towels. They also cleaned their boots of mud and applied black axle grease from a bucket that stood nearby, in order to give them the appearance of cleanliness. In Auschwitz I, it was possible to keep yourself fairly clean. This knowledge somehow lifted my spirits.

We finally all lined up for our so-called dinner, which consisted of a cup of watery coffee, a thin slice of bread, and a tiny square of margarine. This was my first dinner in Auschwitz I, and it did nothing to fill my stomach, which cried out for more.

I stared at the bread. "Should we eat all of it, or keep some for tomorrow?" I asked my father. I longed to shove the whole thing into my mouth, but I wondered if there would be more the next day. We had not yet begun to work, and I already knew that our bodies would need food for whatever work was to come. My father, uncle, and I talked over whether we should save some of the bread.

"But where will we keep it?" I finally asked. There was no place in our bunk to hide food like this. And I already sensed that the other starving prisoners would do anything to steal from us if given the chance. Hunger drove people to do things that they might not normally do. I stared down at the slice of bread and finally wolfed it down, grateful for the small amount of food, knowing it was not nearly enough to nourish my body.

12

- - - - - -

"If you break your stone,

you will be shot."

The next morning, the order for the roll call, which in German was known as *appel*, sounded early. We all rushed downstairs and lined up in front of our barracks like soldiers in an army. Twenty rows of five people spread out so that the count could proceed smoothly. I extended my left hand sideways to touch the shoulder of the person next to me and my right hand straight ahead to touch the back of the person in front of me. We had to line up in this manner as quickly as we could or the Kapos would beat us. As the SS soldier in charge of our barracks arrived to begin the count, the Kapo yelled, "Caps off!" I grabbed the cap off my head and held it tightly.

We had to stand at full attention while the numbers were counted by an inmate who was in charge of reporting the count to the SS officer on duty. On a good day, when the totals added up, *appel* would take anywhere from an hour to an hour and a half. When the numbers were off, we could stand there for hours while they checked the barrack, looking for someone who might have died in his bunk overnight. The body of that poor prisoner would be brought outside and held up so the count could be completed. Then the Kapo would shout, "Caps on!"

Once the guards were satisfied with the numbers, each work unit was marched to the gate, led by its Kapo, and surrounded on all sides by guards and German shepherds. There was an all-male orchestra that played marching music as we left for work in the morning and again when we returned in the evening. I had to admit that I found the music comforting and inspiring, and I wondered how this beautiful music could exist in this otherwise dreary and scary place. I picked up my feet to the beat of this uplifting music. As we marched out at a fast pace, I felt as if we were a group of campers going off to work instead of hungry and terrified prisoners.

After the ordeal of *appel*, it felt good to be able to walk and watch the scenery outside the camp. We passed a bakery operated by inmates. They were baking bread for the camp, and there was a whirlwind of activity as the prisoners loaded loaves onto trucks. The air around the bakery was thick with the enticing smell of baking bread. It made my stomach growl with hunger. Each day we passed this bakery on our way to work, and each day my stomach growled more than it had the day before. The tiny slice of bread we received each night teased my stomach into wanting more. I envied the fellows who loaded the bread trucks, because I believed they would be able to steal bread when no one was watching. They would surely never go hungry like me.

As we walked on, we reached an area where both sides of the road were covered with mustard plants as far as the eye could see. They were waist-high and the flowers on top were bright yellow. We finally stopped at a satellite camp that was called Budy. Here were dozens of barracks, horse stables, all kinds of farm equipment, and many prisoners doing different types of work. I was ordered to begin loading scythes—large hand tools that could slice through crops—on a flatbed cart.

Once the flatbed cart was full of tools, we pushed it to the edge of the field of mustard plants, where we were ordered to begin cutting the plants down. Choosing the right scythe to use was so important. There was a sudden frantic rush to grab one that wasn't too heavy but could still do the job. Fifty men scrambling to grab one of these knifelike tools was quite dangerous! We also received a stone to sharpen the blade of our scythe.

"Make sure you do not break your stone!" This order came from the Kommandant who ran Budy. "If you break your stone, you will be shot on the spot." This officer was another man to be feared.

We quickly got to work. The strongest men led, setting the pace for the rest of us to follow. My father, my uncle, and I were familiar with scythes because my grandfather had used one for cutting hay. We knew the tool was most effective when it was held at a certain angle and at an even height. My father began to cut first. I followed, and my uncle came after me. It was gruelling physical work, and our Kapo watched constantly to make sure that we kept up a steady rhythm. It was a hot day, and the sun burned down on us. I was parched with thirst, and there was no water available at the site.

I had used a scythe at home for half an hour or sometimes an hour at most. But here, I cut continuously for four hours until we stopped for lunch. I felt like my back was breaking. The palms of my hands had large blisters and some had already burst. Yet despite all our hours of work, it looked as if we had hardly made a dent in the mustard field. My spirits sank.

But in that moment, I caught sight of a boy in his twenties from my hometown. We made eye contact, but we had no opportunity to speak. Suddenly, he came around and slipped me a piece of bread. I was so grateful for his unexpected kindness, and it helped me continue to work.

After four hours of labour, we were allowed to stop for a thirty-minute lunch break. A horse-drawn cart brought canisters of soup, and we each grabbed a metal dish and lined up in single file to be served. When my turn came, I received a ladle of a foul-smelling mixture I had never before seen in my life. It had bits of mouldy bread floating on top, with pieces of mustard stalks mixed in. It was disgusting and I gagged. This would be impossible to eat!

"You will eat, no matter what," my father said as he watched me turn my nose up at the soup. He practically forced it down my throat, knowing that, as bad as it was, I needed it to survive.

Nearby, an SS guard pulled out his lunch, a sandwich that he washed down with a drink from his Thermos. I imagined there must have been good coffee inside, and I watched enviously, swallowing some soup and trying to stop myself from throwing up. The SS guard's German shepherd lay close by, perfectly still. He was a beautiful dog, and I found myself thinking of Farkas and wondering where he was. Was he still guarding our house? Was he missing me as much as I was missing him?

After lunch, we continued working. By now, my body felt as if it were going to break.

"I don't know if I can do any more," I whispered to my father.

"You must keep going, Tibor," my father urged when

he saw how discouraged I looked. "The Kapo will beat you if you appear to be weak."

I knew we had to avoid beatings at all costs. Beatings might mean that we couldn't work at all, and that would lessen any chance of survival.

"Put one foot in front of the other," my father encouraged, "and think positive thoughts about surviving all of this."

I thought about the relationship I'd had with my father all my life, a relationship that had been strained by his strict discipline and high expectations of me—expectations I had not always been able to meet. But here in Auschwitz, I was beginning to realize that my father's disciplined approach would be the key to helping me stay focused and determined. I knew I could depend on his emotional support, and I felt so thankful that he and my uncle were here with me. Without them, I realized, I would never have survived past the first two weeks in this horrible place.

I put my head down and kept on working.

13

"I used my boots as a pillow."

The days marched on, back-breaking, monotonous days. Each day began with a hike of several kilometres to Budy, accompanied by the band that played us out of Auschwitz. We worked for eight to nine hours each day and then marched back to camp, always checked by the Kapo, who watched to make sure we were in step. As we neared Auschwitz, I could hear the camp orchestra starting to play again, and this perked me up, helping me regain some strength and lifting my spirits. To me, the music was the only humane and normal thing in the camp. The music gave me hope.

At the end of every day, when we arrived back in Auschwitz I, we rushed to our barracks, washed and cleaned our striped uniforms and boots, and lined up for our dinner of watery coffee, a thin slice of bread, and a tiny square of margarine. To this day, it amazes me to think how we could survive on so few calories. As time went on, however, our bodies began to break down due to the lack of nourishment. Some inmates contracted scurvy, a disease caused from a lack of vitamin C in one's diet. Vitamin C comes mainly from fruits and vegetables, none of which we had in Auschwitz. I don't know how I managed to stay as healthy as I did, but it gave me a feeling of accomplishment that I could remain relatively strong.

We had to eat our dinner very fast and get back outside to line up for *appel*. Standing in that line after so many hours of hard work was a terrible punishment. I thought about what my father had said about thinking positive thoughts, thinking about surviving. So, I imagined that I was a tree with deep roots in the ground, and this image was the anchor that kept me standing upright. I was still so grateful to have my father and uncle by my side—my guardian angels. They helped keep me tough. Some men fainted from standing so long. If they fell, they were beaten and forced back into a standing position. If they could not stand, the prisoners on either side of them had to hold them up until the count was complete.

That first night, after cutting mustard plants for hours, I went to the small infirmary to get some bandages for my blisters. A doctor put some iodine on my wounds

My family in 1940: Alfred (left), my mother, me, my father, and Eugene.

and gave me a roll of paper bandages. I was worried that I wouldn't be able to work with my injured hand the next day. The wounds did take a while to heal, but eventually my hands became as hard as leather.

Every night, at about 9:30 p.m., a gong sounded, indicating that everyone had to be in their bunk. The camp was closed for the night. Anyone found outside after that could be shot from the guard towers. Once we were in our bunks, the lights were turned off. This was the only time in the day that I took off my boots. I used them as a pillow, tying the shoelaces to my wrist so no one would be able to steal them from me in the night.

As I lay in my bunk, I thought of my clean and comfortable bed at home, which now seemed a million miles away. I could see my family, the faces of each one of them. I didn't want to forget what they looked like or what they had taught me. But at the same time, I knew that if I let my thoughts get too carried away, I would become too sad and that might make me weak and helpless. I already knew that you couldn't survive in this place if you were weak. So, I made myself stop remembering my family members. Only then could I go to sleep. All the men around me groaned aloud in the night. And as I drifted off to the sounds of their whimpers and snores, I wondered what the next days had in store.

14

"My father said we needed to split up."

One day a couple of weeks later, we were out again on our work detail. By now, all the mustard plants had been cut down and we were given a new job to dig trenches. One group of prisoners dug at the edge of a swamp, while a second group, including me, waded into the swamp to dig channels that would direct the water into another ditch.

The sun was burning hot, and my boots and pants were soon wet and full of mud. Despite all the water around us, we weren't able to drink it because it was filthy and filled with bacteria that could have killed us. I had thought that working in the mustard fields was awful, but this was much, much worse.

During the lunch break, my father, my uncle, and I sat together as a family, just as we did every day. The Kapo, Heinrich, must have noticed this, and somehow he didn't like the three of us always being so close. He came over and stood right in front of my father.

"Who is that person next to you?" Heinrich asked, pointing directly at my uncle.

"He's my brother," my father replied.

"And that one? Who is he?" This time, Heinrich pointed right at me.

"My son."

I had been wary of Heinrich since our first day in Auschwitz I, when I had seen him wielding his club. I was about to learn how right I was to be afraid.

"Get your tools and get back to work!" Heinrich suddenly yelled.

I had taken my boots off during lunch to try to get the mud out of them, and so I was barefoot when the Kapo barked out his command. I rushed to get my boots on while still sitting on the ground, but I wasn't quick enough for Heinrich, who expected his orders to be followed without a second's delay. He raised his club and began to hit me. I thought my bones were going to crack, but I didn't make a sound. I had noticed that when the Kapo was beating others, he would become even more brutal if they yelled out from the pain or begged him to stop. I don't know how I did it, but I managed to keep my mouth clamped shut, praying that by staying silent, he would finish up with me more quickly and move on. When the beating finally ended, I grabbed my tools and my boots and ran into the swamp to continue working. I was sore and had welts all over my body, but thankfully, nothing was broken.

Heinrich was not done with us. The next day, he went after my father, giving him his own terrible beating. When I saw my father's pain, I was angry and frustrated that I could do nothing to help him. Later that day, when we returned to camp and were in our barrack, my father and my uncle came over to me.

"We need to do something to avoid Heinrich," my father said, still nursing his wounds from the beating.

I nodded. My uncle stood grim-faced next to my father.

"Heinrich is probably attacking us because he's afraid that by being together, it will only make us stronger as a family unit," my father continued. "He hates that thought."

I knew in my heart that my father was right.

"First you, then me, and Uncle Eugene will be next. And then Heinrich will start all over again. We won't be able to survive these beatings if they continue."

"What can we do?" I asked, swallowing hard. I had a feeling I knew where this was going, and I didn't like it one bit.

"I think we need to split up for our work details," my father said.

I nodded again, my heart sinking.

I don't know how my father and uncle managed to do it, but two days later, they were assigned to a different work detail while I remained with Kapo Heinrich. Being in a new work detail meant that my father and uncle were also moved to a different barrack.

For me, this was the start of a new chapter. At fifteen and a half years of age, I was completely on my own during the day, and I had only a few hours at the end of the day to spend with my father and uncle before evening lockdown. How would I be able to manage without my guardian angels on either side of me? I didn't know the answer to that. But I did know that there was nothing I could do about any of this.

I had to show my father that I could manage, that I had it in me to survive on my own.

After a few days, my feet began to suffer from the constant work in the swamps. Standing in the water all day made my boots soggy, and I couldn't remove them until I got back to my bunk. By the morning, when my boots had dried, it was very difficult to get my feet back into them. I had to force them, and I could no longer use the piece of rag that I had previously wrapped around my feet in place of socks. My heels rubbed against the boots and my feet were soon a bloody mess. With constantly bleeding heels, I had trouble walking. I didn't know how to deal with this problem, which was very worrying, because without healthy feet and the ability to walk, you were in big trouble. Every morning, I woke up and focused on making it through the day. My father had always told me to put one foot in front of the other and think about surviving, and this was the advice I repeated to myself constantly.

After a while, my heels miraculously healed, and I was able to wrap my feet with a piece of cloth to protect them. I didn't want my father to worry, so I never told him about my injured feet. But soon, one thing after another began to wear down my body and my strength. I was covered with painful sores from the lack of vitamins. My body was screaming for food, but there was none to be had. I thought about it during the day and dreamed about it during the night. I remembered how much I had hated my mother's tomato soup with rice when I was a kid back home. I would have given anything for a bowl of that soup now!

I could see men all around me who had given up. They walked around with glazed eyes and stopped following orders. They were beaten, but it made no difference. And finally, they were ordered to be killed in the gas chambers. The truth is that they had given up on themselves and on life long before that final order. I was determined not to become one of those glassy-eyed men. There were many times that I faced desperate situations in the weeks and months that followed, but I continued to follow my father's advice: put one foot in front of the other and think only about survival.

I made a deal with G-d that if I survived and made it out of this place, I would be a very good person. I would not want much in the way of material goods. A piece of bread, a potato, and a glass of milk would be a dream come true.

15

- - - - - -

"I tucked the second egg

into my armpit."

Other work details followed, each one worse than the one before. Sometime in June, we were marched to another satellite camp, where we were ordered to enlarge the surrounding electrical fence. It was our job to place the many cement posts in holes. The fence wires would then be connected to these posts. The posts were enormously heavy, and it took three inmates to lift one. It was crushing work that weighed down on my entire body, especially my shoulders. Each time we were ready to move a post, we counted to three and then lifted it up all together. We carried the post down into a ditch and then up the other side and placed it into a pre-dug hole. If one of us stumbled, we all would have been crushed by its weight. All the while, the Kapo in charge would shout, "Faster! Faster!"

By the time we placed the first post, my body felt as if it would give out, and I wondered how I could possibly lift the next one. It took superhuman effort and concentration just to stay upright and walk in a straight line while this tremendous weight threatened to push me to the ground. We were assigned to this job for three full days under the strict supervision of the Kapo, who watched us for any sign that we were slacking off. My body screamed for water, food, and rest. When our thirty-minute lunch break came, I savoured every drop of the watery soup and each moment of shade under a birch tree.

One day in late June, we were marched out to work to the sound of the orchestra, as usual, and I wondered what nasty surprises were in store for me. It was pouring rain that day. I was soaked, and the water ran down my body and into my boots. It was hot and muggy, so the rain actually felt good. I took off my waterlogged cap, twisted it, and drank the water I was able to wring from it.

Another time, we returned to the mustard field in Budy, one of the satellite camps. The fields were dry, and there was a mountain of white powder at one side. We were ordered to load it into baskets, which quickly became heavy because the powder was saturated with rainwater. As soon as we had a full basket, we were directed to the fields we had drained just a few weeks earlier and were told to spread the chalky substance on the ground. I held the basket on my thigh with my left hand and used my right hand to scoop out as much powder as I could to scatter across the field. When the basket was empty, I walked back and filled it up, again and again.

We learned that the powder was lime, a poisonous chemical substance that could be used as fertilizer. The lime seeped out of the basket and went through my jacket, burning and eating away at my skin. I wanted to scratch my body all over, but that only made it worse. My skin became more irritated and began to crack and bleed. I wondered how I was going to survive this job, which would last for about a week, until we finished the spreading. By then, the skin of the fingers on my right hand was eaten away and the skin on my kneecaps was gone. I was terrified that the chemical would destroy my body.

At the end of each day, I tried to wash it out of my pores, but we had no ointments or treatments to help our skin heal. This was a job that would normally have been done using some sort of equipment, to avoid direct contact with the chemical. However, the Nazis didn't care about our health and safety. They didn't care if we died, and many prisoners did die during this time. We meant nothing to them.

For the final three days of this work detail, we worked near some duck ponds. I could see the ducks and hear them quacking. At the end of each of the three days, as a form of entertainment, the Kommandant ordered us to run into the water with our clothes and boots on, and then he told the guards to release their dogs. Those who couldn't run fast enough were clawed by the dogs. I was aware that when I hit the water, other prisoners would pile on top of me and I could be drowned, so I always tried to outrun the others. On the last day, after jumping into the water, I swam into some nearby reeds and found a nest with two large duck eggs. This was a miracle discovery. I knew that eating the eggs was dangerous. If someone saw me, I could be punished or even killed. But the eggs were such a temptation, and I didn't care about the consequences. I immediately cracked one open and sucked it out. It tasted wonderful and gave me a boost of strength that my body so badly needed.

When I heard the order to get out of the water and line up for counting, I grabbed the second egg and tucked it into my armpit. I was determined to bring it back to camp for my father and uncle. This too was risky. As prisoners were marched back to camp, the SS sergeant in charge of the gate would watch each prisoner carefully, searching for any suspicious behaviour. If he detected something, he would yell to the prisoner to stop and lift up his arms. If the man had anything hidden in his armpit, it would immediately fall out. Those prisoners would be punished. In spite of the danger, the prisoners who managed to find scraps of food would always take the risk of trying to smuggle them into the camp. I decided to take this risk as well, wanting to share this find with my father and uncle. But during the march back, the egg broke. I was devastated to lose this gift. I realized how things had changed.

Not so long ago, losing a single egg would have seemed like nothing to me. Now, this loss was almost too much to bear.

One day after coming back from work, I saw my father and my uncle waiting for me inside the gate, just as they always did. My work unit was always the last to get back in the evening, and my father and uncle never failed to wait for my return. A few times, they snuck me a piece of bread or a potato they had managed to get from a work detail. They always shared food with me, even though the risk of punishment was great. We were constantly on the lookout for anything that might improve our chances of survival.

There was a special building in Auschwitz that was called Kanada. All the belongings of the newly arriving prisoners were collected at the railway platform and stored in this building. Inmate workers sorted through the items. Sometimes food was used to hide valuables—a coin might be hidden in a bread roll, for example. Inmates who worked in Kanada were allowed to eat the food but were forbidden to take gold, jewellery, or money.

On one particular day, my father's unit was working near the Kanada building when a girl from our town recognized him. She had been working inside Kanada, and while sorting through some suitcases, she had found a chunk of bacon, which she managed to slip to my father wrapped in a rag. It was a totally unexpected act of kindness. My father smuggled the bacon into Auschwitz I under his jacket, and then he slipped it to me while we were standing in a huddle. My uncle blocked the view so that nobody would see this handover.

I was surprised to find myself holding this chunk of bacon in my hand. And I was even more surprised when my father said, "Tibor, hide this bacon in your barrack and make sure you eat a little piece of it every day."

We were an observant Orthodox Jewish family, and according to our dietary laws, we were not permitted to eat pork of any kind. I couldn't believe my father was giving me permission to break this important law. And not only was he giving me permission to break the law, he was actually pushing me to do so.

"It's a matter of life and death, Tibor," my father added, noting the shocked look on my face. "You must choose life!"

It was impossible to store anything in my barrack, but I managed to dislodge one of the ceiling tiles above my bunk, creating a small space where I hid a few odds and ends, including pieces of rag. I stashed the bacon in a space behind this tile. For the next several nights, I waited until everyone was asleep, and then, when I was certain that nobody would see me, I removed the tile and pulled out my secret treasure. And then I chewed off a small piece of the bacon. I could actually feel the energy flowing into my body. Every night, I had another bite, and I am positive that this little bit of bacon gave me the strength I needed to face the next day.

16

- - - - - -

"Tell the world what happened here."

The word *selection* sent fear through my fellow prisoners and me.

I had come to understand what the gas chambers were after learning about the death of my mother, siblings, and other family members. And I knew about bodies being burned in ovens after that. When we worked in the fields on humid days, the giant chimney spewed smoke in the distance. Sometimes, the ash from the chimney would float toward us and rain down in flakes that settled on us like blackened snow. I had heard that the Nazis convinced newly arriving Jews to enter the gas chambers by telling them they were going to have a shower. That might have worked with those who were just arriving in Auschwitz. Those of us who had been here for some time knew better.

Selection was the ongoing process of determining who among us would be sent to the gas chambers and who would live on for some period of time until the next selection. Selections could happen at any time of the day or night. Prisoners were paraded in front of SS doctors in charge of the selection. The doctors checked to see who still looked healthy enough to work and who was too weak or sick. If you were stopped during the examination and your tattoo and barrack numbers were recorded on a clipboard, that meant you were going to your death. I told myself that I would rather die by throwing myself against the electric fence than be selected to go to the gas chambers.

One night in July, we were awakened from our sleep by the sound of Kapos yelling, "Selection! Leave your clothes in your bunk and get down to the ground floor!"

They herded us onto the street and forced us to run to a nearby building, where SS doctors were waiting to examine us. We filed by them in a single line while they studied each prisoner, checking carefully to see who looked sickly, unfit, or too pale, who walked with a limp or stood straight and tall. I nearly froze, fear jolting through my body like electricity. I needed to look strong and healthy. I needed to look alive and capable of physical labour. My life depended on that.

Suddenly, the person in front of me was stopped, and his tattoo and barrack numbers were recorded on the clipboard that the SS doctor carried. I knew this was a death sentence for him. But I quickly realized that this was an opportunity for me to get away. While the SS doctor was busy recording this poor prisoner's information, I simply slipped by him and kept moving toward the exit of the building. I didn't pause for one second, knowing that if I was stopped, the doctors might inspect me more carefully and send me to my death. Miraculously, no one noticed me, and I breathed a sigh of relief when I walked outside. I was lucky this time.

Back in my barrack, I couldn't get to sleep. As relieved as I was for myself, I couldn't stop wondering what had happened to my father and my uncle, who were in a different barrack than I was. How had they managed during this selection? I would have to wait until the morning to find out.

The next day, I ran to their barrack, but they were not there. I thought the worst must have happened. But I couldn't find out anything more at the time, because I had to join my unit for *appel* and then work. The day was unbearably long for me. All I could think about was my father and uncle. I tried to convince myself that they had just been picked to join another work unit. I tried to believe that they were okay and that their numbers had not been written down. I hoped for the best, but inside, I knew that I was lying to myself.

That evening, when I returned from my work detail, I rushed to their barrack again. They were still not there.

"Have you seen my father, Zoltan Eisen? Or my uncle, Eugene Eisen?" I asked the prisoners who occupied the bunks next to them.

No one knew where they were.

No one had seen them.

I ran to a fenced-off holding area where I knew that the SS kept the selected prisoners until they were ready to be taken to the gas chambers. I saw many people milling around inside this area, and frantically, I called out the names of my father and uncle. Seconds later, they appeared from within the area and came forward to meet me at the barbed-wire fence. My face lit up with joy, but within seconds, my heart sank, knowing these were likely our last moments together. I opened my mouth to say something, but no words came out.

What could I possibly say?

I couldn't offer hope.

There was none.

"Move away from the fence!" The angry voice of a guard in the tower reached me. "Move immediately or I will shoot you." He aimed a gun in my direction.

My father reached through the wire and placed his hand on my head. He uttered a prayer, the same one he had said to bless my siblings and me every Friday before the Sabbath. "May G-d bless you and keep you safe. May

He be gracious unto you. May He turn his countenance to you and give you peace." Then, he stared deep into my eyes and said, "If you survive, you must tell the world what happened here. Now go."

I was devastated, and my heart sank faster and deeper than before. How was it possible that I would never see my father again? I would not have survived here up until now without his protection, the bits of food he shared with me, the moments he advised me and looked out for me. How could I go on in this evil place without him and without my uncle? My two guardian angels.

I began to walk away, turning at the corner of the building to take one final look at both of them standing behind the barbed wire. The feeling of sadness and loneliness simply overwhelmed me.

I knew in that moment that soon I would be the only living member of my immediate family.

17

"I had not laughed once in months."

For days after saying goodbye to my father and uncle, I walked around in a haze, barely able to think or move. I felt more alone than ever. But I had little opportunity to continue mourning them. Work never ended in Auschwitz, and I had to remain strong and alert. It's what my guardian angels would have wanted.

One day, the SS marched us to an area of land that was full of bushes and large tree stumps. They ordered us to clear the entire space and level the soil because they wanted to use the land for growing grain and mustard. Although the hot sun beat down on us, the fresh air felt good, and it didn't seem that this work would be as tough as our previous jobs. The tract of land we were clearing was large, and we had space to move around. And the bushes protected us from constantly being watched by the Kapo or the Kommandant. The guards and their attack dogs were spread out around us, and while I could not see them, I knew they were patrolling in a circle. At one point, I thought of trying to escape and wondered what it would be like to run as far from Auschwitz as I could. But it was all a dream. Escape from this place was impossible. We were surrounded by electrified barbed wire and watched by patrolling soldiers in watchtowers. Vicious dogs were ready to tear us apart. If anyone was caught trying to escape, the punishment was death by hanging in the central square.

"Work faster!" the Kapo shouted, driving us to pick up the pace.

At noon, a horse-drawn cart brought canisters of watery soup, and we had our usual thirty minutes of rest. That's when the jostling and shoving began as prisoners tried to find a good spot in the lineup. Being close to the front was important. The soup that was ladled out in the beginning was thicker and more filling. It was thin and watery for those at the back of the line. If you got to know the person ladling the soup, and he liked you, then he might dig deep to the bottom of the soup cannister and spoon out some of the bits that had settled there. I hated the pushing and shoving in the soup line, and the feeling that we were like hungry animals desperate for food. It was degrading to be forced to fight over this disgusting soup. I told myself that if I survived, I would never, ever stand in line for anything again.

One day, during a lunch break, I heard the whistle of a train a short distance away. We were on a flat ridge overlooking the train tracks, and I was eager to see what was coming our way. When the train drew nearer, I saw that there were many flatcars being pulled by the locomotive. Each flatcar carried two tanks, and on each tank, there were soldiers in black SS overalls. They were singing, laughing, and waving as they went by. I wished that I were free to sing and laugh, as they were doing. I had not laughed once in the two months that I had been in this harsh and ugly place.

The next day, we were working in a deep hole that we had dug. The soil from the hole formed a large mound next to it. We thought the mound hid us from being seen by the guards, and we began to relax and slow our pace of work. It was a big mistake. What we didn't realize was that the mound of dirt also prevented us from seeing if anyone was approaching. Suddenly, two of my co-workers jumped up and started to work again at a furious pace. I wasn't as quick. I felt a blow on the back of my head. At first, there was no pain. I felt dizzy and my ears buzzed. But when I tried to pick up my shovel, something warm began to drip down my neck and I saw that it was blood. I turned around and locked eyes with an SS guard who had come up over the mound and was standing behind me. I realized that he had hit me with the butt of his gun. His eyes were cold, and his mouth twisted into an evil sneer. I thought I was looking at the devil.

I collapsed as blood continued to pour from the back of my head. The other prisoners hauled me out of the pit and threw me into a nearby ditch to keep me out of the way until the end of the day. It was impossible to work anymore. I tried to stand but my legs gave way. I thought of my father's last words as he had stood behind the barbed wire before being led to his death.

He had said, "If you survive, you must tell the world what happened here." I realized that I wasn't going to make it. I wouldn't fulfill my father's last wish. My death would mark the end of the Eisen family.

When our lunch break came, I couldn't even stand up to go and line up for soup. No one brought me anything to eat. It was as if the others also knew I was dying and had written me off. Meanwhile, the blood continued to ooze out of the wound, and eventually, the under-Kapo, a man named Stasek, approached. He tore off a piece of my prisoner garb and wrapped it around my head. The bandage eventually stopped the bleeding, and I was thankful to him. Without his help, I probably would have died on the spot.

By now, the Kommandant had probably received a report that our unit was down one prisoner. He came to have a look at me. I thought he would pull his pistol from his holster and shoot me on the spot. Instead, he signalled with his right hand, his finger pointing up in a circular motion. I knew this meant that I was going to become smoke that would rise up and out of the chimney, just like all the smoke from the others who had been gassed and burned. I shivered with fear and was overwhelmed with helplessness. How could I prepare myself to face the gas chambers? I had always sworn that I would run to the electrified fence and throw myself against it rather than be gassed. I couldn't even do that. My legs would never support me. I actually began to wish that the Kommandant *had* put a bullet through my head.

That's when I began to think of my family and wonder how they must have felt facing their death. I imagined my mother fighting for her last breath in that horrible gas chamber. I imagined her desperately trying to protect my three siblings. I wondered if the end would come quickly for me, and I imagined meeting my family again in some other place. I wanted someone to take care of me, to help me, protect me, and comfort me.

I knew that no one would save me.

At the end of the day, after my work unit had lined up and was counted, all the tools were loaded onto a two-wheeled cart, and I was thrown on top. As the unit began to march back to camp, I was highly aware of what I saw and heard around me, especially the sound of the camp orchestra that always played to send us out to a work detail and to welcome us back at the end of the day. The music had been an important part of my camp life. Like the coffee, and soup, and bit of bread that we received every day, the music had nourished me. I believed it was the last time I would hear any of it.

The cart was left in a shed with all the tools in it, and two inmates took hold of my arms and dragged me a short distance through the gates of the camp. I was surprised to see that under-Kapo Stasek, the man who had stopped the bleeding on my head, was there waiting for me. He directed the inmates to take me to the hospital in barrack 21. I was left there in a hallway near the operating room.

18

"The taste of anaesthetic was

in my mouth."

Next, I was carried into the surgery room and placed on the operating table. My jacket, pants, and boots were removed, and someone put a mask on my face and gave me ether, a sweet-smelling chemical that immediately put me to sleep. I awoke sometime later. My head was bandaged from some kind of surgery that I must have had, and I was groggy from the anaesthetic that had put me out, which I could taste in my mouth. But more than anything else, I was surprised to discover that I was still alive!

I looked around, noting the sick and skeletal-looking patients who were lying in beds all around me. Something told me that I needed to leave this place as soon as possible. Although I was dizzy and weak, I managed to get out of bed on my own. I was determined to walk around the ward by holding onto the bed frames. But I was still too shaky. Eventually, I had to lie back down to gain strength.

A short time later, the chief surgeon in the hospital, a prisoner named Dr. Tadeusz Orzeszko, came in to check on me. He was a tall, strongv-looking man with short blond hair and steel-blue eyes. There were several other doctors in barrack 21. But Dr. Orzeszko was the one in charge.

"It looks good," he said to one of the other doctors as he examined the wound on the back of my head. He looked calm and confident as he touched the area and studied the stitches. "I think it will heal well."

Then he instructed the other doctor to put on new bandages. I was given a pair of white cotton pants and a white shirt. These were the clothes worn by the doctors under their white coats. I felt clean and presentable for the first time in months. The daily rations were the same here in the hospital, but I was also given a hot, thick cereal, which was reserved for hospital patients.

I stayed in that ward for three days. I knew I had to regain my strength and heal as quickly as possible. All patients who were still in the ward after three days were deemed to be unfit to work and would be sent to the gas chambers. On the morning of my third day, I was still

A photo of Dr. Tadeusz Orzeszko, taken on his incarceration at Auschwitz I, July 29, 1943. (Courtesy of The Archive of The State Museum of Auschwitz-Birkenau in Oświęcim)

weak and knew it would be impossible for me to return to work. The SS sergeant in charge of barrack 21 arrived with men who were ordered to lay each patient who was going to be removed on a stretcher and place his identity card next to him. I was one of those who was placed on a stretcher and carried down the stairs to the main hallway. Trucks waited outside to take me and the other sick patients away.

Once again, I knew my life was in danger. Once on that truck, I would be driven to the gas chambers and that would be the end. How many times could I come close to death and still survive? I felt as if I had run out of chances. But to my surprise, the chief surgeon, Dr. Orzeszko, was waiting in the main hallway when I was carried down. When he saw me, he held his hand up to the stretcher-bearers.

"Stop," he ordered. He took my identity card and helped me get up. "Come with me," he said. I was startled by this turn of events but followed obediently as he led me to the prep room next to the operating room. There, he turned to me.

"You have a new job," he said, handing me a lab coat and telling me to put it on. "From now on, your job will be to clean and prepare the surgical room. You are the one who will help ensure that surgeries are well-organized and run smoothly."

I was still in a daze, still recovering from my own surgery, and still astonished that Dr. Orzeszko had stepped in to help. My life had been saved once again, and while I didn't know exactly what my new responsibilities would be, I was determined to do this job as well as I possibly could.

19

"The operating room had only the most basic equipment."

There was a long list of things I had to learn to do in the operating room. The person who trained me was a young Polish medical student who was serving a one-year sentence as a political prisoner. He was due to be released in three days, and I would be his replacement. I watched him carefully during his remaining days on the job. I wasn't afraid of having to keep the surgical room as clean as possible, but it was scary and overwhelming to see medical instruments and other equipment that I had no idea how to use.

The prep room had two sinks with hot and cold water where the surgeons washed before surgery. There was a huge machine for sterilizing sheets, gowns, masks, gloves, and other items, and a separate sterilizer for instruments, along with a timer that I had to set to know how long to keep the instruments inside. The shelves in the cupboard were neatly laid out with clamps, scalpels, hammers, saws, syringes, needles, and scissors of all shapes and sizes. There were two work tables to gather items before the surgeries. The storage cabinets were filled with supplies, such as paper bandages, cotton balls, cleaning supplies, disinfectants, brooms, and other odds and ends. The operating room itself had a basic operating table with an overhead light, several floodlights, and a cupboard where medications were stored. I was in charge of learning the purpose of each piece of equipment and preparing whatever was needed for surgeries, following the doctors' orders.

As overwhelming as the tasks were, I was determined to succeed at my job. I knew my life depended on my performance.

My workday started at 7:00 a.m. and usually lasted for twelve hours. I followed a strict and precise routine. I started my day by sprinkling talcum powder on the floor of the prep room and the operating room and then standing on two round rags and moving my feet around in circles to polish the linoleum until it shone. I picked up the freshly washed linens, gowns, and masks from the laundry barrack next door and packed them neatly into three containers. Next, I loaded the containers into the steaming machine, closed and bolted the lid, and turned on the high-pressure steam so that the linens were sterilized. Finally, I assembled the instruments for that day's operations.

When the surgeons arrived at 10:00 a.m., I had the water boiled for their tea and I took a fifteen-minute break before the first operation began. The patients were lined up on a bench in the hallway, and I called their numbers in the order that was given to me. While the surgeons were washing up, I helped the patient onto the table and covered him with a sheet. Then I went to the prep room to help the surgeons tie their gowns and masks and to hold the surgical latex gloves so they could put their hands into them. Sometimes I had to administer ether—the same anaesthetic that had been used to put me to sleep for my surgery—to those who were being operated on. I instructed the patient to count backwards from thirty to one as the ether took effect. My final job was to bring the surgical instruments to the operating room and lay them out before the surgeons.

At first, I was uncomfortable watching the surgeons work, particularly when I saw them make the opening cut. But I quickly became used to the sight of blood in the operating room. When the surgeons finished their job, they came out through the swinging door into the prep room and removed their gowns and gloves. Once the patient was taken away, it was my job to immediately mop the floor and clean and disinfect the operating table. I had to be quick about it. Within thirty minutes, another patient would be laid out on the table for their operation. I had to keep the prep room and the operating room clean and ready so that the doctors could continue to do their work.

After the last operation of the day, the surgeons left and I was in charge of putting the rooms in order again for the next day. I gathered all the bloody sheets, gowns, towels, and masks and delivered them to the laundry barrack next door for cleaning. My next task was to sweep and mop the operating room floors and clean the walls, if necessary. Then I had to wash all the instruments: the scissors, syringes, scalpels, and needles that I kept separated to avoid cuts to my fingers. When all the instruments were clean, I laid them out in a line. They had to be completely dry before I placed them into the cupboards in an organized line. The scalpels also had to be sharpened on a fine stone.

When the prep room and operating room were clean and ready for the next day, I put out the lights and went upstairs to my bunk in a room I shared with the doctors and the orderlies. I was dead tired at the end of every day, but it always took me a while to fall asleep. I realized that the surgery ward was, in many respects, a scam designed to show how "well" the Nazis looked after their patients. These patients were destined to be killed eventually, because in most cases, they were beyond help. But the surgeons still took their jobs seriously and did the best they could for their patients under impossible conditions. The doctors were themselves prisoners, and they also had to please the SS officers in charge of the camp.

I was lucky, I realized, to be working in barrack 21 alongside these dedicated surgeons. I was fed and clothed, I had meaningful work, and I did not have to endure the back-breaking tasks of the work units that went out into the field. My head injury, which had been devastating, had actually turned out to be my lucky break.

20

"Grab a loaf of bread from the pantry."

I marvelled at Dr. Orzeszko's ability to perform complicated surgeries under the most difficult conditions, using whatever techniques and equipment he could pull together. Once, an older man was brought to barrack 21 for surgery. He was accompanied by two men from the Gestapo—the Nazi police—and, from listening to his conversation with Dr. Orzeszko, I gathered that this man was doing important work for the Nazis.

The doctor looked at his X-rays and told me to fetch and sterilize some equipment, including a stainless-steel handsaw and cutting pliers. The patient was infected with tuberculosis, a serious disease caused by germs that are spread through the air. It was known to infect the lungs, bones, spine, brain, and other parts of the body. In this man's case, the disease had infected two of his ribs just above his heart. With his assistant surgeon, Dr. Orzeszko discussed having to remove ten-centimetre lengths of bone from the two diseased ribs using the handsaw and pliers. The doctors looked worried, and they talked together about how they could perform this surgery with their crude equipment. I sensed that this was going to be a difficult operation.

The surgery began well. I stood close by, wiping sweat from Dr. Orzeszko's forehead. But partway through the surgery, one of the patient's veins began to bleed so much that it was clear the man would die if something wasn't done, and soon. That's when Dr. Orzeszko turned to me and gave me what sounded like the strangest instructions.

"Tibor," he said. "Go to the pantry beside the prep room and take a loaf of bread."

Why on earth was he instructing me to go and get some bread in the middle of this difficult operation? It made no sense.

"When you have the bread," the doctor continued, ignoring my puzzled expression, "go and find an orderly. Use the bread to bribe him to come here to the operating room."

The instructions still did not make much sense to me, but I followed the orders, as I always did. I took a loaf of bread from the pantry and went to find one of the orderlies, also a prisoner working in barrack 21. The man eyed the bread hungrily as I faced him. I held the loaf out to him, telling him that it was his if he would follow me to the operating room. He didn't ask any questions. He nodded, and I gave him the bread and lead him back to Dr. Orzeszko.

"Good," the doctor said when the orderly appeared. "Now, I want you to lie down here on this stretcher next to this patient."

The orderly's eyes widened, but again, he didn't say a word. He had his loaf of bread, and now, he needed to obey the doctor's orders.

"I'm going to perform a blood transfusion," the doctor continued once the orderly was lying down.

He held up a tube with a needle at either end and explained that he would insert one of the needles into the orderly's hand and one into the hand of the patient. Then, he would direct blood to flow from the orderly into the patient, replacing the blood that the patient had lost. It sounded simple, but I knew it was complicated, and dangerous! The doctor's assistant operated a valve to control the blood flow. If it flowed too quickly, it would put the patient into shock. We didn't even know if the blood types for the two men matched! If they didn't, that would also kill the patient.

Luckily, everything went well. Dr. Orzeszko watched carefully as the patient's heartbeat stabilized and his colour returned to normal. All of us in the operating room were relieved. The veins were tied, the clamps were removed and counted, and the incision was stitched up. The surgery was a success. The orderly left the operating room, the patient was put back into the ambulance, and he and the Gestapo men who escorted him left the camp.

I learned an important lesson that day about how to act in situations you're unprepared for and how to use the resources at hand. I was in awe of what Dr. Orzeszko had been able to do with a handsaw, cutting pliers, and a loaf of bread. It was only one example of the many times that the doctor used his cunning and skill to save lives.

21

-- -- -- --

"The Americans are coming

to free us!"

The months rolled on, and by September 1944, American bomber planes flew over Auschwitz on an almost daily basis. Rumour had it that the planes were targeting ammunitions installations located close to the camp. If the Americans could destroy these installations, then they could limit the number of bombs and bullets that the Nazis had for their own attacks. Whenever a plane flew overhead, a siren sounded to alert the entire camp population that a bombing raid was approaching, and all work units that were close to the camp had to return immediately. The SS did not want work units out in the open where, in the confusion of heavy bombing, some prisoners might try to escape.

Once all the work units were inside the camp, the main gate was locked and the electrical fences were activated, once again to stop anyone from trying to escape in the confusion that might follow.

A single advance airplane would fly overhead and drop a flare to mark the place for the planes to release their bombs. Within minutes, we could hear the drone of the bombers' powerful engines, and a moment later, we could see the planes. They were impressive! The planes flew in squadrons, evenly spaced, in a massive display of force.

The ground shook like an earthquake with every bombing raid, and shrapnel flew through the air. Sometime in September, there was a heavy bombing raid while we were in the middle of an operation. We had to stop our work, and I opened the windows in the surgery and prep room so that the glass would not shatter from the exploding bombs. Outside, shrapnel and shards of glass were landing all over the camp. But I didn't care about that.

Keep dropping those bombs, I whispered under my breath. *The Americans are coming to free us.*

Despite the destruction, I was filled with hope and believed that the Nazis would soon be defeated and punished for all the evil deeds they had committed. When the bombers left, the all-clear sirens sounded, I closed the windows and the operation continued.

Later, I learned that the United States Air Force bombed during the day, and the British Royal Air Force bombed throughout the night. The camps had anti-aircraft guns, which were placed near the outer limits of the electrical fence. These guns fired up at the squadrons of bombers. But the bombers knew what they were doing and stayed mostly out of range of the guns. Once, a bomber was hit by one of these anti-aircraft guns, and I watched in dismay as the plane started to spin out of control and spiral toward the ground. I thought the entire crew on board would be killed. But suddenly, I saw parachutes fill the sky and I knew in my heart that the crew had managed to get out alive.

By the fall of 1944, the Americans, the British, and other Allies ruled the skies over occupied Poland, and I never saw a single German fighter plane attack the Allied bombers. I longed to be as free as the pilots above, whose movements were not controlled by evil forces.

One day, while I was preparing for the next patient to be operated on, the door to the prep room opened and an SS officer I did not know entered and began speaking to Dr. Orzeszko. The officer ordered him to clear the operating room of other patients and make space for several injured SS soldiers who were being brought in by ambulance. I learned that the officer's name was Dr. Fischer, the official doctor to the SS. He was the one responsible for making sure no contagious diseases that might make the SS soldiers and staff become sick developed in the camp. I also learned that the operating rooms in the SS hospital that would normally have been used for these soldiers had been bombed and were out of commission. That's why Dr. Fischer had to use the operating room in barrack 21.

"I will be the one who performs the next surgeries," Dr. Fischer announced as several men were wheeled in and lined up in the hallway. "Dr. Orzeszko will be assisting me."

I followed the doctors into the hallway as they began to check the condition of the injured SS men to assess who was in the greatest need and who would be operated on first.

"You," Dr. Fischer said, pointing at me. "Cut off their uniforms and prepare them for surgery."

I stared curiously at these soldiers. Most had shrapnel wounds in their legs, chests, and arms. They moaned in pain as I cut their uniforms away. I was suddenly aware of how frail these killers looked lying on their stretchers, injured and completely helpless, while I, a fifteen-year-old Jewish prisoner, was in charge of them. These were the soldiers who had taken our belongings when we arrived in Auschwitz and had ravaged the bodies of the dead. They had beaten and abused us. Yet now they were weak, while I was the stronger one. That realization filled me with a sense of satisfaction that I had not felt in a long time.

Dr. Fischer unbuckled the belt that held his pistol and handed it to me, along with his jacket. He then sat on a stool to wash up for the operation, while I controlled the water temperature. He asked me to cover his riding pants with towels so they would not get wet.

"What's your name?" he asked as he ran his hands under the water.

I told him my name, and then answered him again when he asked where I had been born and my date of arrival in Auschwitz.

"And your family? Where are they?"

A warning bell went off in my mind.

Why was he asking me about my family when he must have known what happened to the transports like mine that had come from Hungary? Something inside of me cautioned me not to say too much.

"I don't know where they are," I finally replied. While it unnerved me to be asked these questions, I tried to look calm.

When Dr. Fischer had finished washing up, I held up the sterilized gown so he could put his hands inside. He was over six feet tall, so I had to get up on a stool to tie the gown around his waist and neck. I also tied on his mask and held out the latex gloves while he put them on.

Finally, I placed the surgical instruments in the sterilizing machine. Normally, I would sterilize these tools for twenty minutes to ensure they were clean and free of germs. But at the last minute, I decided I would only disinfect them for five minutes. I had no desire to use safe cleaning methods on these evil men who would have killed me in an instant given the chance.

It was my small act of rebellion and the only way that I could think of to fight the enemy in that moment.

We operated on the SS soldiers for two days in the surgical room of barrack 21 until the bombed-out SS hospital was back in action.

22

- - - - -

"It was impossible to get out of Auschwitz alive unless someone helped."

I t was a well-known fact among the prisoners that it was impossible to get out of Auschwitz alive unless someone helped you. My head wound, which at first I thought might kill me, had become an opportunity for survival. It had saved me from those terrible work details that were wearing down my body at a rapid pace. I worked in the operating room for six months, and my structured daily routines allowed me to survive away from the severe hard labour and the threat of the SS guards and the Kapos. But even that opportunity to work in the operating room would not have been possible without the immediate first aid I received from under-Kapo Stasek, who stopped the bleeding on my head and arranged for me to be sent to surgery in barrack 21. Without his help, my story would have ended in a scrubby field of tree stumps. I also owed my life to Dr. Orzeszko, who had not only operated on my wound but had also taken me off the stretcher that would have sent me to the gas chambers. Dr. Orzeszko was a dedicated and skilful surgeon who was respected by his peers and the Polish prisoners of Auschwitz I. I owed my life to him.

One day, a short while after I started working in the operating room, Dr. Orzeszko opened a pantry door and showed me shelves loaded with food supplies, including loaves of bread, salami, onions, potatoes, carrots, salt and pepper, and a large cooking pot. There was more food here than I had seen since I left my home in March 1944, and my jaw dropped open in astonishment. Dr. Orzeszko told me how to prepare a stew with all of the food items and how to use the steam sterilizer as a kind of pressure cooker.

"I want you to be the one who cooks these meals for us," Dr. Orzeszko said. I nodded as my mouth watered, thinking of the smell the food would make as it cooked inside the sterilizer. Of course, there was always the worry that the aroma would give us away, so I knew that this kind of cooking had to be done after all the operations were finished for the day and the SS officer in charge of the barracks had left for the night. That's when I began to prep and cook the meal. I had it ready in less than an hour. The first time I cooked a stew, I ate so much that I felt as if my stomach could burst. I couldn't believe that I was eating this feast here in Auschwitz! The leftovers were locked in the pantry and eaten the next day. I knew that I was one of the few privileged prisoners who was able to enjoy meals like this. The extra calories made a huge difference in my overall health and strength, and this food was also key to my survival.

I learned that Dr. Orzeszko, like other Polish political prisoners, was allowed to receive small monthly care packages containing food and other supplies. He was also allowed to receive and write one letter per month. I was happy that the doctor could receive these supplies and could write to his loved ones and feel their love in return. But it also reminded me that Jewish prisoners like me did not have this same privilege. There was no one left to send us these precious gifts.

It was the end of December 1944, and Christmas and New Year's were about to roll in. I joined the surgeons and doctors of barrack 21 at a celebration that included political prisoners, barracks elders, Polish tradespeople, German and Austrian Kapos and under-Kapos, and SS Kommandants of the different work units. I figured there were approximately a hundred people assembled in the room, which had been decorated with pine boughs and streamers and posters that said "Merry Christmas" and "Happy New Year." The mood was festive, and the atmosphere was warm and welcoming. Tables sagged from the weight of food, which included salami and other meats, cheese, and bread, along with alcohol and other goodies. I did not feel like celebrating anything, but the food definitely lifted my spirits.

As the guests all sang songs, I gazed around the room, watching the faces of the various groups of people and trying to figure out what they were thinking. There were the Polish prisoners, whose faces were lit up with hope, as if they believed that the war was coming to an end and they would be reunited with their families. The SS officers looked uncertain and a bit confused, as if they wondered what was in store for them in the future. The Kapos in the group, those who had beaten and tortured Jewish prisoners like me for years, looked almost sad, as if they were about to lose their positions of power.

And me? I was still afraid that the Nazis would kill us all before we had a chance to leave the camp. Unless I was liberated, there would be no happy ending for me. Perhaps the war was nearing its end, but freedom, real freedom, still seemed a million miles away.

23

- - - - -

"There was a new feeling of urgency in the air."

The Sonderkommandos were Jewish inmates who were forced to work at the gas chambers. Their job was to remove the bodies from the gas chambers, cut off the victims' hair, and pull out any gold fillings from their teeth. Then they would carry the bodies to the ovens that were inside a building called a crematorium. There were four of these large buildings with ovens inside. Each crematorium had a huge chimney that spewed the smoke we saw nearly every day.

The Sonderkommandos probably had the most gruesome job that any human being could have. And as if their work itself wasn't bad enough, members of the Sonderkommandos were killed every sixty days and replaced by new arrivals. The Sonderkommandos were eyewitnesses to the crimes that the Nazis were committing, so they had to be eliminated. The Nazis wanted no one around who might one day report on their activities.

On October 7, 1944, Crematorium IV was blown up in a planned revolt by members of the Sonderkommandos. They had made crude explosives from gunpowder, which they'd gotten from women inmates who worked in one of the factories. The Sonderkommandos also prepared Molotov cocktails, which were simple bombs made by filling a bottle with some kind of flammable liquid, inserting a wick, and then lighting the wick before throwing the bottle. The Sonderkommandos threw Molotov cocktails at the SS, killing several of them, and then they blew up the crematorium. In the chaos that followed, the Sonderkommandos broke out through the gate and ran toward the edge of the camp. Guards began shooting at them, and large backup units of the SS were organized and sent after them. The SS shot down most of them.

Of the approximately six hundred Sonderkommando inmates involved in the rebellion, only six managed to escape from the camp into the nearby forest.

As punishment for this uprising, the inmates of Auschwitz were made to stand at *appel* all night long. Many simply dropped and died from exhaustion. As I stood with my fellow prisoners, I was not only drained of energy but also scared of other consequences that might follow. When we were finally dismissed, I was relieved to go back to the operating room to continue my daily duties.

But it wasn't over yet. The SS officials immediately began an investigation to try to find out how the Sonderkommandos had managed to get hold of the explosive powder. Each factory in Auschwitz made a different and specific kind of powder. The SS had evidence that led them to one factory in particular where hundreds of women were working as slave labourers. Eventually, the SS were able to single out four young women, who were brought to one of the barracks in Auschwitz I to be questioned.

We didn't hear any more news until January 5, 1945, when the entire camp was ordered to assemble in the main square in front of the gallows in Auschwitz I. SS guards were also lined up to form a barrier between the thousands of us who had gathered and the gallows. There were four nooses hanging from the wooden posts, but I had no idea who the victims would be. Finally, the guards brought out the four women. Their hands were tied behind their backs, and their faces were bruised from the beatings they must have suffered during their questioning. But they held their heads high as they walked to the platform. I marvelled at how unafraid they looked. Just before their deaths, each woman spoke out loud and said the same thing to those of us who watched.

"Be strong and courageous," they called out.

I was in awe of their bravery and heroic deeds. And I wished that we could all jump into action and do something to rescue them. As one large group, perhaps we could have helped. But the truth was that we were all too weak and broken down by then to do anything more than look on and feel the shame of our inability to act.

As soon as the hangings were complete, the SS units waded into the mass of prisoners, yelling and trying to move us all back into our barracks. The Nazis were sending us the message that, despite this act of resistance, they were the ones still in control. We were at their mercy, with no energy or weapons to fight back.

But something changed in Auschwitz after that public hanging. There was a new feeling of urgency in the air, as if the Nazis realized that they may be on the losing end of this war and needed to cover up the proof of their crimes. It appeared as if the entire Auschwitz system was beginning to break down.

Many factories closed, and the machinery from these factories was transported back to Germany. Military trucks were loaded with clothing, blankets, and other items from the barracks where these things were stored. The SS piled medical documents and registration cards in front of the barracks, then poured gasoline on them and burned the evidence. These fires continued burning for many days and nights. We heard rumours that the SS planned to blow up the three remaining gas chambers and crematoria. I was relieved to hear this. I knew that as long as these engines of death were working, I was at risk of being sent to one of them. Our daily activities slowed greatly and our workload in the operating room was down by almost fifty percent. Suddenly, I had lots of spare time. With less to do and fewer responsibilities, I worried that I might have outlived my usefulness as a slave labourer. The Russian Red Army was approaching to free us, but I wondered what the Nazis would do to us as our rescuers drew near.

24

"We are leaving Auschwitz."

ike many prisoners, I lived in constant hope that the Russian Red Army would arrive in the next week or two, we would be freed, and our nightmare would finally be over. That was not to be. On January 18, 1945, a rumour spread that we were going to be leaving Auschwitz. We didn't know where we would be going. We didn't know where this was all going to end. We didn't know whether the Nazis were going to kill us or set us free.

That same night, the SS walked through the camp shouting orders. "Line up!" they bellowed. "You are all moving to another camp. Line up immediately!"

I had no time to think about what that might mean as twenty thousand of us were ordered to form ourselves into rows of five with our arms hooked together. As we left the camp, we were each given a chunk of bread. I didn't know how long this journey would be or how long this bread would have to last. Outside the gates, the SS guards and their attack dogs positioned themselves on either side of our enormous column. Fires burned all around us, casting an eerie glow. I had only a light jacket and cap, but thankfully, I also still had my sturdy boots. Their soles were worn down to almost nothing. But they were better than the wooden clogs that many prisoners had. I could still walk in my boots, but those clogs were virtually impossible to walk in.

It was bitter cold and there was a lot of snow on the ground. My body was in a full sweat despite the cold that was seeping through and dampening my thin jacket and pants. My feet were soaked in minutes from the deep snow. My only added protection was from a paper cement bag I had managed to grab from a construction site we passed. I ripped holes in the bottom and the two sides and pulled the bag over my head like a vest.

We set out at a fast pace and were constantly prodded to move faster because the SS did not want the column to stretch out too far, making it difficult to guard. Those who fell out of the column were immediately shot; the SS were determined not to leave any prisoners behind. I was on the outside left of my row. The five of us realized that we needed to march in unison, with our arms hooked together, in order to conserve our strength and keep up with the pace. We could not waste energy on anyone weighing us down because it was difficult enough to carry our own bodies.

We marched like this for three days, sleeping for short periods in the snow-covered forest. As the sun rose over the snow on the third day, the landscape seemed strangely beautiful. There were thousands of inmates in front of me and thousands behind me. All around us, the SS guards cursed and shouted.

Where are they taking us? I wondered. *What is the point of all this?*

At noon, we left a forested area and came to a village, where I could see houses with smoke rising from their chimneys. I thought about the warmth inside those homes and imagined normal people having their lunch. How wonderful a cup of tea would have tasted right then! All I could do was grab a handful of snow, shove it in my mouth, and pretend I was being fed.

As we entered the village, we were ordered to squeeze closer together because of the narrow streets. The guards watched carefully for anyone who might try to escape. In the chaos of our rushed departure, I had lost contact with all the Polish doctors of barrack 21. I thought of those doctors now. They could have slipped away easily because they were in their homeland and spoke the native language. I could not take this risk.

Instead, I had to march on, and as I did, more people fell away from the column and the gunshots became more frequent.

Later in the day, as we neared a crossroads, I saw a farmer sitting on a sled pulled by two beautiful horses. The bells on their harnesses were ringing as they waited for the large column to pass. I remembered those cold winter mornings from my childhood, when farmers came to town and I would jump on the runners of their sleds to hitch a ride to school. Would I ever hitch a ride like that again? I grabbed another handful of snow and continued to put one foot in front of the other. Surely, I thought, we would stop soon. While I was determined to carry on, the dreary days and dark nights were extremely difficult, and my spirits were at an all-time low.

In the afternoon of the third day, we came to a large, abandoned farm, where the Nazis told us we would spend the night, our first real stop since leaving Auschwitz. The farm had many stables and storage barns, and it was wonderful to rest at last. The straw on the floor of the barn cushioned my body. I buried myself in a pile of this heavenly smelling straw and went into a deep sleep. The next morning, I awoke to the guards shouting, *"Raus! Raus! Line up!"* For a moment, I thought about hiding in a pile of straw, but I knew I would be shot on the spot if discovered. As it turned out, I was right to have worried about this. As we lined up in formation, the SS guards moved through the stables, shooting into the piles of straw. Anyone who was hiding was killed.

We had already marched for three nights, and the only food we'd had was the piece of bread we were given before we left Auschwitz. It was long gone. I only learned much later that this long, endless march would become known as the Death March. The name was fitting. All around me, prisoners died in the snow or were shot when they couldn't keep up. I was weak and light-headed from lack of food. I tried to keep my mind focused on positive thoughts, just as my father had always told me. But my spirits were low, and any hope of freedom that I may have had was flooding out of me.

25

"I felt as if I were in an icebox."

On the fourth day, we arrived at a town called Loslau and were marched to the railway station. There we found a long line of forty to fifty open flatcars waiting for us. The SS guards ordered us to climb inside. They packed more prisoners on these flatcars than I ever imagined was possible. The flatcars had no roofs, and the walls were made of metal and were icy cold. Everyone pushed to get a spot near the middle of the group for warmth. The train started up, and as the locomotive built up speed, the wind swept over my head, piercing the cold even deeper into my body. I felt as if I were in an icebox. The SS guards had perched themselves on several cabooses that were located between the flatcars. From there, they could easily watch over us and shoot anyone who dared to try to escape.

We travelled only during daylight hours because at night the smoke and the cinders of the locomotive would have been a giveaway for low-flying Allied fighter pilots, who bombed anything that moved on the rails. Overnight, we stood at railway stations, where the SS units patrolled up and down the line of flatcars so that no one could escape. At one point, I thought of a book I had once read about a passenger train called the Orient Express. It was known to be one of the grandest and most expensive trains in operation. I tried to imagine what it would be like to sit in a train like that. But I couldn't distract myself for long with these dreams. The reality of where we were always came rushing back to me.

Standing in the cars was even harder than marching because we were in such cramped quarters. To make it worse, in the mornings, before the train took off again, the SS guards and their officers were served breakfast from the kitchen car. I could smell food being cooked, and it was a terrible tease. The SS soldiers were being fed while we were dying from starvation. *Where are we going?* I wondered over and over. *How many more days will this harsh journey last? Will I be alive at the end of it?* We had left Auschwitz on January 18, and now it was January 25: seven days of unbearable travel, standing up, chilled to the bone, without food or toilet facilities, and bodies piling up all around me. The only thing I had put in my mouth were a few handfuls of snow and the snow-flakes that I caught on my tongue to hydrate myself. I was barely hanging on. Heavy snow was coming down on us, and I felt as if we were zombies, wet to the bone.

At one point, we passed a railway station where I could just make out the name Pilsen in the early morning light. That was a city in my country of Czechoslovakia. I felt a sense of hope as I realized that I might be close to home. But suddenly, I heard a commotion. There was a bridge ahead of us, and on that bridge were several peo-ple throwing chunks of bread into the flatcars below.

The SS guards yelled out, "Do not throw bread! These are Jews!"

But the people ignored them. Finally, the guards shot at the bridge with their submachine guns and the peo-ple ran away. I was too far away to receive any bread. But knowing that there were still kind and caring people who were willing to help us and feed us boosted my spirits and gave me new life.

On the seventh day, the train stopped, and we were finally ordered to get off. In the distance, I could see a railway bridge spanning a wide river, and someone said that this must be the Danube River. That meant that we were probably either in Germany or in Austria. It didn't matter either way. Up ahead, I could see large chunks of ice floating down the river, and my first thought was that the guards were going to line us up on the riverbank and shoot us all, dumping our bodies into the water. Why else would the train have stopped here and not proceeded across the bridge? But as I got closer, I had my answer to that question. The bridge had been badly damaged by Allied bombings. Railway ties were twisted or missing, causing wide separations in the footings. It was not possible to get over the bridge by train. Instead, we were ordered to march across on foot.

Getting across was a tricky operation. One missed step and you'd end up in the icy river below. That would be the end of you. I had to pace myself and focus on keeping my balance, which wasn't easy because prisoners were grabbing at one another to stop themselves from falling. There was no margin for error. Many prisoners tumbled through the missing spaces and into the fast-flowing water below. I was among the lucky ones to make it across. There, the guards ordered us to line up in formation once more, and we were marched forward. Ahead of us, I could see a town, and we were told to tighten up our lines as we came closer to it. A roadside sign told us we were in a place called Mauthausen.

26

"Shivers of fear flowed through me."

My first impression of Mauthausen was that it was a beautiful town. There were lovely homes and storefronts with sparkling clean windows and delicate lace curtains. Each building was about three stories high, and there were decorative wooden ornaments on the outside. It was unbelievable to think that there were people inside these buildings and homes living in safety and comfort, while my fellow prisoners and I were living in misery, filth, and danger. I longed to be inside one of those homes. I thought I could die happily if I could just have a hot bath.

While we marched through the town in the centre of the road, we passed three young women, each pulling a child in a sleigh. The children were all bundled up and wore knitted toques and scarves. They had rosy cheeks and bright eyes. But they gazed at us with looks of horror on their faces. We were dirty and in rags. A foul odour followed us like a stray dog. The children stared while the women looked away. I thought of the people in Pilsen who had thrown bread to us off the bridge. Those people had been kind while these women turned away at the very sight of us.

We continued marching through Mauthausen, passing a large granite cliff on one side. Inmates in striped garments were hammering at the stone with chisels. This sent shivers of fear through me. I knew we were going to be put to work, but I knew that I could not handle this kind of back-breaking task. We continued marching and finally came to the top of the road. There I saw the fortress-like entrance to Mauthausen concentration camp. I recognized the tall guard towers on either side of the gate with soldiers inside holding machine guns. It was a scary sight.

Inside the camp, I could see that Mauthausen was overflowing with inmates who, like us, had been brought from other camps in occupied Poland. We were told to stand outside in the freezing floodlit square for hours until several Kapos took charge of the crowd. They ordered us to undress but to keep our shoes. And then we waited in the cold while groups of one hundred people at a time were sent to the showers. When it was finally my turn, I stood under the flow of warm water, feeling it wash away the dirt and smell from my body. I had not had a real shower in months. But it was over too quickly, and we were pushed back out into the freezing cold, where we continued to stand throughout the night. Despite the shower, I could feel the chill creeping deep inside me, and I began to flap my arms, hitting my upper body to keep my circulation going. I did this for hours without stopping. Many inmates dropped to the ground during the night and froze in the snow. Finally, the next morning, those of us who were still alive were led to the barracks.

The barracks overflowed with prisoners. There were at least a thousand people in each barrack. I was furious. Of all the hardships I had suffered, being packed together this way, sitting on the floor, intertwined, was frightening and shameful. We were a sea of bodies pushed up against one another. I sat this way for two days until the Kapos shouted at us to get up and get out of the barrack. We were outside again in the bitter cold and had to form in a single line to receive our clothes: striped pants, a top, and a cap.

"You'll be going to another camp," one Kapo shouted.

I was happy to leave this terrible place and hoped I'd never see it again. It had been ten days since we'd left Auschwitz, and I'd still had nothing to eat or drink. I realized that getting food and water would be the only thing that might keep me alive. Without it, I would soon be gone.

We were marched out of the gates of Mauthausen, across the same dangerous bridge we had crossed days earlier, and down to the railway station, where we were crammed into boxcars. The locomotive started up and we were on the move again. A few hours later, the train slowed and eventually came to a stop. The guards opened the doors of the boxcars and shouted, *"Raus! Raus!"*

A sign told me that I was in a railway station in a town called Melk.

27

- - - - -

"Here I am, in another camp,
all alone again."

It was either February 1 or 2, 1945, when our transport arrived in Melk. By then, I had lost track of days and time. The guards forced us to march uphill, through the town, and into the Melk concentration camp. After lengthy discussions between the SS guards and the Kapos, they divided us into groups and assigned us to various barracks. I was directed to a barrack that was already home to a number of Russian prisoners of war. We managed to talk to one another using a mix of Russian, Slovak, and German.

"Which camp have you come from?" one prisoner asked.

"Where were you born?" another asked.

The most urgent question came from someone else. "Do you know what's happening with the war? How is it going?" The only news I could give these prisoners was that when we left Auschwitz on January 18, I'd heard the sound of heavy artillery coming from the east.

"It must mean that the Russian Red Army is not far away," I said. The men nodded eagerly.

Despite the presence of these Russian prisoners, I felt more alone than ever. Here I was in yet another prison camp, wondering how I would adjust and manage to do the work I knew was to come. I was terrified that I would have to work outside in the bitter cold, and I knew I couldn't survive if that were the case. I told myself that if I could just manage to get through the months of February and March, spring would arrive, and surely by then, the Russian Red Army would emerge from the east to end this ordeal. Maybe by the spring, I would be freed. I vowed I could do it—survive until then. But there were so many things to worry about, and I needed to be ready to face all the challenges.

That evening, I received the first bit of food in ten days, a piece of bread and something that looked like coffee but tasted nothing like it. The ration was welcome, but it did not fill my stomach. The only mattress I could sleep on was so filthy that I chose instead to sleep on the wooden bed planks, covered by a dirty blanket. As I lay my head down, I had a fleeting memory of the upstairs ward in barrack 21 of Auschwitz with its clean bunks, clean blankets, and hospital duties that I could manage. In the hospital, I'd felt as if I had been part of a group of professionals who were helping our fellow prisoners. Strange as it sounds, I suddenly felt as if I were missing Auschwitz. How was that possible? How could I miss a place that had meant death to so many, including my family members? In that moment, all I believed was that Melk was going to be a very dangerous place.

The next morning, we were woken up at 5:00 a.m. and given a cup of tea. We lined up in the square and then were marched down to the railway station, and once again, put into boxcars with the doors locked. We travelled for about an hour and then were ordered to get out. I found myself in a large fenced-in area with many sheds that stored machinery. I could see six large bomb-proof railway tunnels that were built into a mountainside and a locomotive pushing fifteen to twenty boxcars into one of them. I learned that four of these tunnels were already in full production making aircraft parts. The other two tunnels were still being built.

The SS divided us into groups, and a man in a black cap and white overalls led my group to the last tunnel, which was still under construction, and to an area where the stone was being drilled.

"Your job is to drill into the rock using this," he shouted, pointing to a large air drill. We were meant to be drilling a stairway to the top of the tunnel in order to shape the outline of the ceiling. But I could barely lift the drill, and when I pushed the handle to start it, the vibration shook my body so violently I nearly dropped it. The sound was ear-piercing. As I started to drill, I worried that the rocks above my head would come crashing down on me, crushing me instantly. I didn't know how long I would be able to do this work!

I managed to get through two days, but after that, I couldn't bear this job any longer. I approached the man who supervised me and asked to be moved to another job. It was risky to ask for such a favour. Why should I be shown any special treatment? Thankfully, the supervisor agreed, and I was given a new job to pick up the broken drill bits that had piled up in the tunnel and take them to the blacksmith's workshop for welding. This move was another lifesaver. I could handle the work. There was always a red-hot fire burning in the furnace of the black-smith's shop, making it feel cozy and warm.

28

"Will I make it to seventeen?"

The blacksmith was a Russian prisoner of war named Misha. Once I got to know him better, I asked him if he would make me a holder to carry a number of broken drill bits at one time. He agreed and made me a carrier for six drill bits. It was approximately a half a kilometre from the tunnel to the blacksmith's shop. Even though it was heavy to carry the holder with so many drill bits, it made my job easier as I didn't have to make so many trips back and forth. I also figured out how to pace myself so that there were always enough replacement bits at the site for broken drills. That meant that I could spend more time inside the warm blacksmith's shop. One day, Misha even helped me by giving me a pot and telling me to fill it with clean snow, which he melted on the fire for the two of us to drink.

On March 15, I turned sixteen years old. There was no party for me and no celebration. But I remembered the promise I had made to myself. If I could just manage to get through the months of February and March, spring would arrive, and maybe by then I would be freed. As the end of March approached and the weather began to get warmer, I could hear sounds of bombing coming from the east. I dared to dream that the end of the war was coming closer. I thought of my home life back in my town of Moldava. At this time in the spring, we would have been enjoying the festival of Purim, celebrating the time when Jews from Persia were saved from being killed under the rule of the Persian king. Purim became a day filled with food and rejoicing for our freedom from oppression. It had been our family custom to share goodies with our friends and neighbours. My mother always made one of my favourite meals: a stew-like dish called chicken paprikash, and she baked delicious cakes. Those celebrations had happened so long ago.

Will I ever see my home again? I wondered. *Will I never make it to seventeen?*

One morning, I woke up feeling sicker than I had felt in a long time. I had stomach cramps, diarrhea, fever, and dizziness. How was I going to manage working when I could barely stand? All I wanted to do was stay in my barrack, curled up in a ball. I didn't care what the consequences would be. But my bunkmates hauled me out of bed and pushed me into a line to receive my breakfast tea. I couldn't even drink it. I barely managed to walk from the camp to the train that took us to work. When I arrived at the work site, I started to collect the broken drill bits from the night before to take to the blacksmith's shop for welding. When I brought them to Misha, I told him that I was sick and couldn't keep anything in my stomach.

"Here," he said, handing me a piece of charcoal to chew. "Swallow this with a bit of water. It will help kill whatever germs are in your stomach."

Then he told me to crawl under a bench in his shop and go to sleep. I ate charcoal and slept for three days. During that time, I gave my meagre food rations to my bunkmates, because I could not keep anything in my stomach. I was becoming weaker and weaker. But on the third day, I suddenly began to feel better! I knew that Misha's charcoal had saved me. Without his home remedy, I would not have survived this illness, and I was grateful for his help.

I was finally able to return to work, but the next day, when our shift ended and we were lining up to be counted, the foreman came running up to the officer in charge and reported that someone had damaged the conveyor belt by cutting out two pieces of leather to use as soles for their shoes. This was a very serious violation. The Kommandant announced that the person who had done this had one minute to step forward. No one did. The Kommandant then ordered the SS guards to pick out every tenth person from the line and bring them forward. They skipped over me by only two people, and I breathed a giant sigh of relief. They marched the selected men a short distance away, and then the Kommandant gave the order to fire.

Ten men were killed to set an example for the rest of us.

I thought about the fact that someone had saved my life by giving me a piece of charcoal.

Nothing had saved these men.

29

- - - - - -

"I had a feeling that the end was very near."

One day toward the end of March, I looked out from the top of the hill in the camp to see groups of military and civilian trucks, along with buggies loaded with furniture and people on foot pulling handcarts. I also saw overloaded trains with people sitting on top and hanging off the sides. All the vehicles were heading west, away from the advancing Russian Red Army.

If everyone was running away, what would happen to us?

I hoped that our guards would simply go away and leave us alone, but that is not what happened. The next morning, we were marched down to the railway station to work as if it were just another ordinary day. I collected drill bits and carried them to the blacksmith shop.

"The Red Army will soon be here," Misha told me. "There's no need to work very fast. You can go to sleep under the bench."

I was awakened a short time later by the sound of shooting. I jumped up and looked out the window just in time to see a fighter plane circling the yard and firing at anything that moved. A locomotive pulling boxcars emerged from a tunnel. The pilot of the plane banked around and fired a stream of bullets at the locomotive. It exploded, and thick black smoke and flames filled the sky.

"It's a Russian fighter plane," Misha shouted over the noise.

When the coast was clear, I took my drill bits and returned to the tunnel. Once again, I had a feeling that the end of the war was very near. When our shift ended, the SS lined us up to be counted as usual, but the evening shift did not arrive. We climbed into the boxcars and went back to the camp, where everyone was talking about the fact that work in the tunnels had paused. I wondered if we would be lined up to leave this place and marched on to some other prison camp. *It would be hard to march again*, I thought. But by now it was April, and the weather was warm. I knew that this time at least, if we were forced to march, I would not have to worry about freezing weather. It was a small encouragement.

The next day's wake-up call came earlier than usual, and this time the entire camp was assembled in the square. We stood for some time and then were ordered to line up in rows of five, after which we were divided into several groups. I followed my group down to the banks of the river, where there were many barges tied to the shore. The SS crammed us into one that carried metal railway tracks. Once the barge was fully loaded with people, the openings were locked with metal covers and padlocked so we could not escape. *If this barge sinks, we're all doomed*, I thought to myself. Then I wondered if they intended to drown us by deliberately sinking the barges. That thought terrified me.

But that didn't happen. Instead, we sailed upriver to the west and eventually docked. We were ordered out of the barges. What followed was several more days of marching, stopping to sleep for a few hours, and then marching some more. Linz, Gmunden, Wels, Lambach. The names of towns passed by as the hours and days moved on. I placed one foot in front of the other and followed those in front of me. One night, I found a couple of potatoes in a farmer's field, the only food I'd had in days. I savoured them and then slept soundly through the starry night.

The next day, we climbed a road that took us to a higher elevation. It was very warm, and the column of men began to stretch out, with many men unable to keep up. The SS gave us one hour to rest. There were pine trees on one side of us, and on the other side, the road dropped off into a valley. The scenery was beautiful, and under different circumstances, this might have been a wonderful outing. When the rest period was over, we marched on and followed the road even higher.

Suddenly, I heard a plane approaching, its roar startling me out of my daze. I panicked that it was going to shell us, and I braced myself for what was to come. The plane began to fire at us, starting from the rear of the column, but it veered off, as the pilot must have realized we were not enemy troops. As it passed overhead, I could just make out the star on its wing, and I knew it was an American plane. We had been attacked by the very army that was coming to free us! Fortunately, no one in our group was killed.

As the plane disappeared into the distance, I thought to myself that if an American airplane could fly that low without being challenged, their army could not be far away.

30

- - - - -

"I looked like a walking skeleton."

As we marched on, we came to a sharp turn in the road, and I saw an amazing scene in the valley below: a beautiful lake called Ebensee, with blue water and houses and trees around the shoreline. I could see soldiers in blue uniforms rowing their girlfriends in boats on the still lake. This site was a complete contrast to the half-dead prisoners around me, and I vowed to myself that if I survived, I would one day experience the pleasure of boating on a peaceful lake. A short while later, we entered the gates of Ebensee concentration camp.

I was assigned to a new work unit, where I was instructed to mix cement and pour it into forms to produce large tiles. Thankfully, we were not forced to work too hard, and it seemed to me that we were simply putting in time while the war wound down. I had a sense that this would be the last camp for me to endure, that liberation could not be far off, but my body was on its last legs.

I looked like a walking skeleton. My boots that had saved my feet all this time had huge holes in the soles and toes. Worst of all, like so many of the other prisoners, my body was infested with lice. It was bad enough that the lice burrowed under my skin, sucking out drops of blood and itching more than I could stand. But the greater danger was that these vermin carried the typhus bacteria from person to person. Typhus was a terrible disease that, if left untreated, would lead to death. Most of the men in my barracks were already sick with high fevers from typhus, and there were no medications or doctors to treat them. Many of them died in their bunks.

Around mid-April, the SS stopped handing out food altogether, and the water system was also shut down. Bodies had been dumped into the water cistern, contaminating the water and making it undrinkable. I was growing weaker and weaker, and my body burned with fever. I slept endlessly, not even realizing the days that were slipping by.

One day, an inmate shuffled into the barracks and made a surprising announcement.

"The SS are gone!" he exclaimed. "There's no one in the watchtowers, and there's a white flag flying at the main gate!"

I couldn't believe what I was hearing. Was it possible that the enemy had fled and our liberators had finally arrived? I gathered what little strength I had left, determined to get outside to see the white flag with my own eyes. In that moment, I felt that getting out of the barrack meant life, and that if I stayed inside, where I was surrounded by death, I too would die.

When I looked up and saw the white flag, I knew that my horrible ordeal had finally come to an end. I felt as if a crushing weight was lifting off my body!

And as I stared at the flag fluttering in the slight breeze, the gate of the prison camp suddenly crashed down—a tank with a white star barrelled through. What a sight it was! Several African American soldiers were sitting up on the turret. I learned that they were members of the 761st Tank Battalion and were known as the Black Panthers. The soldiers' eyes widened as they gazed in horror and disbelief at the sight that greeted them. Thousands of skeletal inmates, me included, were huddled in groups, and thousands more bodies were piled everywhere in heaps.

It was May 6, 1945. I was still alive.

I was finally free.

EPILOGUE

－ － － － － －

April 1998

A re you okay, Grandpa?"
        I turned to look at Amy, my eldest grand-
daughter, who was part of the group of one hundred and fifty Toronto teenagers I was accompanying on
a trip to Poland. It was the spring of 1998, and we were
here as part of the March of the Living, a program that
brought young people to Poland to tour the concentration camps and learn more about the Holocaust.

I was the survivor speaker who would be talking to
these teens, filling in the missing pieces: the sounds, the
smells, and the feelings of this place. It was the first time
in fifty-three years that I was entering Auschwitz, the
place where the Nazis had killed so many of my family

and friends. With no gravesites to visit, this was the closest I could get to their spirits, and I knew it would be a difficult experience for me.

I smiled at Amy, trying to calm some of the concern I saw in her eyes. "It looks different from when I was here," I said.

The towering chimneys that belched smoke were gone, along with the buildings that had housed the gas chambers and crematoria. The SS had destroyed them before they abandoned the camp in January 1945, and the structures now lay in rubble. The birch trees had grown taller, and where once there was mud, green grass now covered the field.

The place looked strangely gentle to me now, and I was struck mostly by the enormous size of the site, the ruins of the barracks, and the barbed wire. A few kilometres away, I saw the barracks where I had spent so many nights, the places where I was forced to stand at *appel* for hours, and the spot where the orchestra played. I remembered the hunger, the fear, the constant exhaustion. But I also remembered a few critical moments of advice, small kindnesses, and conversations with my fellow prisoners, and the camp hospital that became such an important part of my story.

I had already spent several years speaking in schools and at other events, telling my story. It had been difficult, at first, for me to stand up in front of an audience and speak. I was nervous. My breathing was rapid, and my heart pounded. But I remembered my father's last wish for me to tell the world what had happened in Auschwitz. And slowly I began to improve my speaking skills for different age groups. Eventually, I was speaking to elementary schools and high schools, universities and colleges. I made presentations at churches, synagogues, libraries, and community centres. Despite the demanding nature of the work, I knew how important being a Holocaust educator and speaker was, and I loved connecting with people across the country. I rarely refused a request to speak. Students often approached me after my talks to make comments, take pictures, or ask for my autograph. I received many letters from young people demonstrating the fact that they really did understand the importance of Holocaust history. That had renewed my spirit.

But standing in front of Auschwitz-Birkenau in 1998 was an emotional journey back in time to a very dark place. Thank goodness, I was surrounded by Jewish youth, the Jewish future, and I was next to my granddaughter. I glanced at her again, realizing that she was sixteen, nearly the same age I was when I had first entered the camp in 1944.

"You've always been so strong," she said. "I can't tell you how much I respect the fact that you have been on this mission to educate as many people as possible about what happened to Jews during the Holocaust."

With my granddaughter Amy for the March of the Living, 1998. This was my first time back at Auschwitz since the war.

My heart swelled when she said that, and I took her arm so that we could enter the camp together.

Being back at the camp filled me with sadness, but it also gave me comfort as I watched Amy place a picture of my lost family members on the ruins of one of the crematoria. I knew my family was with me in spirit. And Amy represented the generations of children and grandchildren who had grown up and thrived following the genocide. I understood how important it was for survivors like me to tell their stories, and to honour and remember the people who were lost.

And as I faced this group of young people and began to speak, I was filled with the hope that this new generation would relate to the Holocaust and its lessons with an understanding of how evil can operate when it is not stopped. It continues to be my hope that the students I meet will combat racism and bigotry wherever they see it, and that they will speak out and make a positive difference in Canadian society.

This memoir stands as my own permanent contribution to this history, and to the memory of my loved ones who were lost to this horror.

Looking at the Book of Names—hundreds of thousands of names—at Auschwitz I. I found my family's names among the many lost.

What happened to Max

after the war?

The African American soldiers who liberated Max in Ebensee were members of the 761st Tank Battalion, attached to General George S. Patton's Third Army. They were known as the Black Panthers. These African American soldiers were still suffering segregation and discrimination in their home states. And yet they were fighting for the freedom and liberation of Jews in Europe. The soldiers were followed into the camp several days later by an American Jeep full of officers who arrived to assess the terrible situation in Ebensee. Their first act was to get rid of the typhus bacteria. To accomplish this, all the barracks had to be burned to the ground.

Max was able to shower and was given clean clothes. He was taken to a hospital tent to be examined and was finally fed. One tragedy of the liberation of Ebensee and other camps was that many prisoners were overfed by soldiers and staff who were too eager to help. Many starving prisoners who ate the heavy meat that was prepared for them died when their bodies could not digest the food. Fortunately, Max received only water, crackers, and powdered milk and slowly began to regain his strength.

He and the other inmates had to go to the camp office and register. They were asked their name, birthdate, place of birth, and where they wanted to go. Max wasn't sure about returning to his home country. But eventually, he boarded a truck heading for Czechoslovakia and Hungary. It took a couple of months for Max to finally make it back to his home in Moldava.

The house was still there, but Max knew that his family was gone, and there was no Farkas to greet him when he walked through the gate. The trees had not been taken care of, and the whole orchard appeared to have been destroyed by retreating Nazi armoured units. It was devastating to think of how much care Max's grandfather had once taken to produce fruit from those trees.

Max missed every member of his family, and he wondered how he could pick himself up and go on after so many losses. But then he remembered his father telling him to tell the world what had happened in Auschwitz. With that in mind, he knocked on the door of his house and opened it to his mother's kitchen. He saw the familiar cabinet where she had stored her dishes. And beside it, he saw a neighbour sitting at his mother's table. The woman didn't recognize Max because his appearance had changed so much. When he told her who he was, she became angry. When he asked for water, she refused and told him to go away.

He had no support system and no one to help him prove his rightful claim to the family home. On top of that, he realized that he was becoming ill. His body was bloated and heavy looking, and it was certainly not due to the small amount of food that he was eating. His chest ached with pain and he could only sit upright, making it impossible to sleep.

He managed to find a former neighbour, Illy, the woman who had tried to take Judit, his baby sister, to protect her on the night that Max and his family were all deported to Auschwitz. She was shocked when she saw Max in his weakened condition and took him in. She described to Max what had happened to his home after his family's arrest. She said that people from town had fought over their possessions. The livestock were captured and removed. She also told Max that the synagogue in town had been vandalized and the Torah strolls taken out of the ark and cut into pieces. She gave Max an envelope with two pictures that she had been able to save after the family home was ransacked. The photos were treasures to Max, and he was forever grateful for Illy's kindness and thoughtfulness.

Max was still feeling sick, and Illy took him to see a doctor, who diagnosed Max with an illness called wet pleurisy, where fluids can collect within the chest cavity and press on the lungs and heart. Max was admitted to a hospital, where it took several weeks for the doctors to treat his illness. Gradually, his body strengthened, and he felt more alive and healthier than he had in a very long time. During this time, he also joined a group called the Mizrachi Organization, consisting of Jewish teenagers who had all survived the war. The leaders of the group helped Max and the other young people begin to adjust to life after the war, to learn how to trust again. It was a long and difficult process.

From another boy in the organization, Max learned that a school for orphans was about to open in the city of Marienbad, not far from Prague. He decided on the spot that he would go and was excited about the opportunity to return to school. The town was located in a beautiful mountain setting. Magnificent chestnut trees encircled the town, and each day at noon and again in the evening, a full orchestra played classical music for two hours at a time. Marienbad became a place of healing, and Max spent the next three years there. He read everything that he possibly could and learned much about the world that he had missed out on. He wanted to learn a trade, and since he had the experience of working in an operating room, sterilizing instruments and preparing patients for surgery, he thought he would like to become a dental technician. He was hired by a local dentist to be an apprentice, earning only a small amount of money but grateful for the learning opportunity.

Eventually, many students who had relatives overseas began to leave the school, and in the fall of 1948, the school closed. This was once again an unsettling time for Max. It felt as if everyone was leaving and he did not know where he would end up. The rabbi at the school contacted a rabbi in Toronto, Canada. This man had helped many survivors immigrate to Canada, and he managed to obtain Canadian permits for all of the students needing passports and somewhere to go. Unfortunately, the plan to leave was stopped when the Communist Party took control of Czechoslovakia. Under this new and restrictive government, Czech citizens like Max could not leave the country. He needed papers to show that he was not Czech, and eventually, he travelled to Prague, where he found a man who was known to prepare false documents. Unfortunately, there were hundreds of people ahead of Max who also needed false papers. The forger told him to leave a picture and come back one month later. Max returned to the forger on numerous occasions to see about the progress of his papers. Each time he went back, he was told the papers were not yet ready.

On his fourth visit back, he was met by detectives who arrested him and accused him of trying to acquire false documents, something that was considered a crime against the government. He was sent to a maximum-security prison. He knew that, if convicted, he would spend many years in prison unless he told the authorities how he had planned to get the papers and who else was involved. Max did not want to sign anything admitting that he had committed such a crime. He spent the next six months in prison and was finally released on May 1, 1949.

Max was still looking for a way to get out of the country. He joined up with a group of Hungarian Jews who had been allowed to leave for the American zone in Austria, and he arrived in Vienna a couple of weeks later. From there, he spent some time in a displaced persons camp, set up to house refugees from Nazi concentration camps. Once again, it took many months for Max to obtain the visa that would enable him to leave the country. He finally received that important document and boarded a ship called the *Samaria,* arriving in Canada on October 25, 1949.

Max imagined Canada as a vast land with open skies and a small population. He wanted to live in the midst of nature, not in a huge city. He arrived in Toronto and was housed with an elderly couple who opened their home to newly arrived refugees like Max. One of the first things he wanted to do was find a job. After three years of training to be a dental technician, he thought he wouldn't

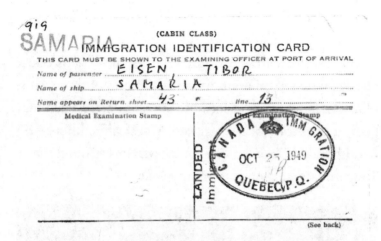

My immigration identification card, which I received when I became a landed immigrant, October 25, 1949.

have a problem finding work in this field. But no dental laboratory would hire him, even though he offered to work unpaid for a few weeks to show them his abilities. He was finally sent to a little shop that was willing to hire refugees. The company was called Art Bookbinding and Novelty Company. It manufactured wedding albums and other items, and Max was hired at a starting wage of twenty-five cents an hour. He was happy to have a job and happy to be able to earn money.

Eventually, Max started his own company related to bookbinding. In 1952, he met and married Ivy Cosman. Together they had two sons, two grandchildren, and four great-grandchildren. He began to work as a Holocaust educator in schools and other institutions throughout the country. He also accompanied many groups to Poland for a trip called March of the Living in order to help young people learn about the realities of the Holocaust and keep historical memory alive. On one of these trips, Max met a man named Johnnie Stevens and learned that he had been one of the African American soldiers who had liberated Ebensee when Max was imprisoned there. They remained friends for many years.

Johnnie Stevens of the 761st Black Panther Tank Battalion and me in New Jersey, 1999. (Courtesy of Doreen Stevens)

In 2015, Max travelled to Lüneburg, Germany, to act as a witness in the trial of Oskar Groening, who served as an SS guard at Auschwitz-Birkenau. Groening was charged with having assisted in the murder of three hundred thousand Hungarian Jews. Max was anxious at the thought of travelling to a German court and having to face this criminal. He felt like the ghosts of the past were with him again. Nevertheless, Max rose to the occasion. He felt drained after his testimony but pleased that his remarks were part of the official record and satisfied that this perpetrator was being held accountable for his crimes.

Sadly, Max passed away on July 7, 2022. He was ninety-three. Throughout his life after the war, he continued to speak about his experiences as a Holocaust survivor, urging young people to be alert to the dangers of hatred and reinforcing the importance of speaking out against discrimination. It was in this way that he fulfilled his final promise to his father: telling the story of their collective suffering so it would never be forgotten.

My wife, Ivy, and my two sons, Edmund (left) and Larry.

My granddaughter Tzipporah Sarah with my great-grandchildren: Yehudit (right), Elisheva (left), and Michael Aharon.

My granddaughter Julie and her son, Jacob.

How I came to know Max

In 2017, I travelled to Poland to participate in a March of the Living program for adults. One of the Holocaust survivors who accompanied us on that trip was Max Eisen. I already knew Max. I have written more than thirty books focusing on stories of the Second World War and the Holocaust, and I have met and interviewed dozens of survivors. I heard Max speak many times to young people and occasionally shared a stage with him. I also interviewed him for a book I wrote about the trial of Oskar Groening. I admired Max greatly. He always appeared so strong and dignified. I was constantly in awe of his ability to connect with young people and share his life story.

On this trip to Poland, we visited Auschwitz-Birkenau, and Max was there with us, standing in front of barrack 21 and telling the story of how he had been saved there by Dr. Tadeusz Orzeszko. When he spoke, he brought the past alive in a meaningful and chilling way.

At one point, as one of our tour guides was filling us in on some of the background history of Auschwitz, I noticed Max moving away from our group. I followed him, past several other barracks, and saw him approach a group of teens who were also there with March of the Living. Without waiting for an invitation, Max began to talk to the teens about his story of loss and survival. I could see that the teens were captivated by his storytelling. And I knew that this was where Max believed he needed to be—with young people, passing his history on to the next generation.

It was a great privilege to be asked to write this adaption of Max's story for young readers. Having written so many books for young people about this time in history, I felt confident that I would be able to adapt Max's story in a way that was appropriate to this new readership. I also felt the weight of responsibility to capture Max's voice as best I could. I knew I would have to simplify his story at times or tone it down and even omit those parts that might be too difficult for a younger audience. At the same time, I was determined to remain true to Max's lived experiences. In those moments where I grappled with how to explain something or how to adapt one of the events of his life, I found myself thinking back to that moment when I saw Max engaging a group of young people in Auschwitz. I asked myself, "How would Max have said this to a group of teens?" And remembering his voice, his dignity, his ability to convey his story in the most straightforward yet most poignant manner, I was able to carry on with my writing.

In Max's memory and in memory of all those who perished in the Holocaust, we share the responsibility to remember this history and, just like Max, to pass it on.

Kathy Kacer
March 2024

TIMELINE

March 15, 1929: Max Eisen (then called Tibor) is born in Moldava nad Bodvou, a town in the eastern part of the country that was once called Czechoslovakia.

1938: Max hears a speech by Adolf Hitler on the radio. Hitler proclaims he will wipe out the Jews of Europe.

October 1938: Hitler's troops march into Czechoslovakia, occupying the whole country.

1940: More laws and rules are introduced to restrict the freedom of Jewish people.

1941: All Jewish males age eighteen to forty-five, including Max's father and his uncle, are sent away to work in mines, forests, and military installations on the Eastern Front.

August 1942: Max and his mother, his siblings, and his aunt Irene are ordered to leave their home. After two weeks of confinement far from home, in a large shed with hundreds of other prisoners, they are released. Several days later, Max's father and uncle are also released from their labour battalion and sent home.

March 1944: During Passover, all members of Max's family are rounded up and deported to Auschwitz-Birkenau. Max, along with his father and uncle, are separated from the other members of the family, who are all sent to the gas chambers.

May 1944: Max and his father and uncle are transferred to Auschwitz I, and they begin forced labour at a satellite camp called Budy. Several weeks later, Max's father and uncle are moved to another work unit and another barrack.

July 1944: Max survives a selection, but his father and uncle are sent to the gas chambers.

August 1944: While on a work detail, Max is beaten by an SS guard and taken to barrack 21 for surgery. He meets Dr. Tadeusz Orzeszko and begins working as a surgical assistant.

September 1944: Max hears American bomber jets flying above Auschwitz.

October 1944: Crematorium IV is blown up by Jews who are part of the Sonderkommandos. The source of the explosive powder is traced to four women working in one of the factories. Two months later, these women are hanged in the central square of Auschwitz. Max and the other prisoners are made to watch the hanging.

December 1944: Max attends a Christmas party in Auschwitz.

January 1945: Many factories in Auschwitz begin to close down and the machinery from these factories is transported back to Germany.

January 18, 1945: Twenty thousand prisoners from Auschwitz, including Max, are marched out of the camp on what becomes known as the Death March.

January 25, 1945: Max arrives in Mauthausen.

February 1945: Max arrives in Melk.

March 15, 1945: Max turns sixteen.

Late March 1945: Max arrives in Ebensee.

May 6, 1945: Max is liberated by American soldiers of the 761st Tank Battalion, known as the Black Panthers.

July 1945: Max returns to his home in Moldava.

1945 to 1948: Max lives in Marienbad and attends a school for orphans.

Fall 1948: The school closes and Max makes plans to leave for Canada.

January 1949: Max is arrested and accused of trying to acquire false documents. He is sent to a maximum-security prison.

May 1, 1949: Max is released from prison.

October 1941: Max arrives in Canada and eventually begins his own business in bookbinding.

1952: Max marries Ivy Cosman. Together, they have two sons, two grandchildren, and four great-grandchildren.

1952: Max begins to work as a Holocaust educator, speaking in schools and other institutions.

April 1998: Max travels to Auschwitz for the first time as a speaker for the March of the Living. On one of his subsequent trips, he meets Johnnie Stevens, one of the African American soldiers who liberated Ebensee when Max was imprisoned there.

2015: Max testifies at the trial of Oskar Groening.

July 7, 2022: Max passes away at the age of ninety-three.

GLOSSARY

——————

Allies: a military union formed during the Second World War. The main members were the United States, United Kingdom, Russia (then called the Soviet Union), and China. These countries came together to oppose the Axis powers led by Nazi Germany, Japan, and Italy.

appel: a daily roll call where prisoners in concentration camps were made to line up in rows to be counted

antisemitism: systematic prejudice against Jewish people. During the Second World War, there were laws and rules in place that officially allowed this prejudice and bigotry to happen.

Auschwitz: a series of Nazi concentration and death camps located near the town of Oświęcim in Poland. More than three million people were murdered there between 1942 and 1944.

Auschwitz I: the main camp and administrative head-quarters of the Auschwitz complex, built in 1940

Auschwitz II: also known as Birkenau. This was a second, much larger section of the Auschwitz complex and was used as an extermination camp.

Budy: a subcamp of Auschwitz set up on a farm, approximately five kilometres from Auschwitz I

crematoria: the ovens where bodies were burned after being gassed. There were five crematoria in Birkenau. In October 1944, crematorium IV was set on fire in a staged uprising.

death camps: concentration camps that were designated as killing centres. The Nazis established six of them to carry out the mass murder of Jews.

Death March: the forced march of prisoners from one camp to another and away from the approaching Allied forces. Most Death Marches took place near the end of the Second World War. Thousands of prisoners died along the way.

displaced persons (DP) camps: camps that were set up after the war to house survivors of the concentration camps who had nowhere to live. The DP camps were run by the UNRRA (United Nations Relief and Rehabilitation Administration).

Ebensee: a subcamp of the Mauthausen concentration camp established in 1943 to build tunnels that would store Nazi weapons. American troops liberated the camp on May 6, 1945.

Einsatzgruppen: the mobile death squads of Nazi Germany. They were responsible for murdering thousands of Jews, mostly by shooting them.

gallows: a wooden structure used to hang someone

gas chambers: the airtight buildings that the Nazis constructed to kill people. Prisoners were marched inside, the doors were locked, and poisonous gas was released.

Gestapo: the security police used by the Nazis to monitor, protect, and wipe out any opposition to Adolf Hitler.

They were also responsible for setting up and administering the concentration camps.

G-d: It is customary in Jewish practice to omit the letter *o* in the spelling of G-d. This is meant to give the name more respect.

Kanada: the name of the warehouses in Auschwitz that were used to store the stolen belongings of prisoners. These buildings became known as Kanada (the German spelling of Canada) because the prisoners believed that Canada was a wealthy country, and the warehouses were full of people's valuables.

Kapos: prisoners in a concentration camp who were assigned by the SS to guard other prisoners. Kapos were often brutal in their treatment of their fellow prisoners.

Kommandant: the highest-ranking position in a concentration camp. All SS guards reported to the Kommandant.

matzah: a thin cracker used in the celebration of Passover. It represents the bread that did not rise when Jewish slaves had to flee Egypt.

Nazi: a member of the National Socialist German Workers' Party. The Nazi Party was headed by Adolf Hitler. It was founded in 1920 and was in power in Germany from 1933 to 1945.

Orthodox: a branch of the Jewish religion. Orthodox Jews typically adhere faithfully to practices that include strict observance of the Sabbath, religious festivals, holy days, and dietary laws.

Passover: a major Jewish holiday celebrating the time in Egypt when Jews fled from slavery

propaganda: art, music, theatre, and film, as well as educational material that was produced by the Nazis and used to brainwash people into believing that Jews were inferior, evil, and should be despised and eventually "eliminated"

Purim: a Jewish holiday celebrated in the early spring. It commemorates a time in the fifth century BCE when Jews were saved from being killed by their Persian rulers. The story of Purim is told in the biblical Book of Esther.

Roma: an ethnic group of people originating in northern India who were also persecuted by the Nazis. Approximately four hundred thousand Roma were killed during the Holocaust.

Russian Red Army: the army of the Soviet Union. During the Second World War, the United States and Russia (then known as the Soviet Union or the USSR, i.e., Union of Soviet Socialist Republics) formed an alliance when they realized that each country needed the other in order to defeat Nazi Germany. The Russian Red Army suffered huge casualties during the war.

Sabbath: a day of rest and religious observance in Judaism. The Sabbath starts at sundown on Friday and continues until sundown on Saturday.

satellite camp: smaller subcamps that came under the command of a main concentration camp. For example, Auschwitz had at least forty-five satellite camps, housing anywhere from a hundred and fifty to over thirty-five hundred prisoners.

scythe: a tool that has a curved blade on a long handle. It was typically used to cut long grass or hay by hand.

Seder: the ceremonial feast that marks the beginning of Passover. The story of the Jews' flight from Israel is recounted during the Seder. Matzah and other symbolic foods are eaten at that time.

selection: the process of determining which Jewish prisoners would be sent to the gas chambers. Sick, weak, or elderly prisoners were considered a burden in the concentration camp. Most women and children were also selected for the gas chambers.

Sonderkommando: concentration camp prisoners, usually Jews, who were forced to work near the gas chambers, removing bodies and burning them in the crematoria. To ensure secrecy, every couple of months, the members of the Sonderkommando were also sent to the gas chambers and replaced with new arrivals to the camp.

SS: Hitler's elite troops whose responsibilities included the persecution of the Jews and the supervision of the concentration camps

Star of David: the universal symbol of Judaism. It has six points. During the Holocaust, the Star of David was a badge, usually yellow, that Jews had to wear on their clothing to identify them. This badge was often used to single them out for discrimination.

synagogue: the place of worship for those of the Jewish faith

Torah: the first five books of the prophet Moses, which contain the laws of Judaism

transport: the transfer, usually by train, of Jews to labour and death camps

typhus: a disease that is spread to humans through fleas and lice. The disease is marked by a high fever and rash. Left untreated, it can lead to death.

under-Kapo: an individual who reported to the Kapo

DISCUSSION QUESTIONS

----

1. As the title *By Chance Alone* implies, there are several instances where luck intervened on Max's behalf. What chance human encounters helped Max survive?

2. How important was hope to Max's survival? Was it hope or simply being lucky that enabled Max and others to survive?

3. Why is it significant that by 1940, Jewish people were required to turn in their radios to the government? What technology do you use to gain information about the world?

4. What kind of propaganda was circulated about Jewish people when Max and his family were living in Hungary? What was the purpose of this propaganda? Are there examples of discriminatory propaganda being used today? How do you challenge this kind of propaganda today?

5. Once Max found safety and a home in Canada, how did he ensure that his voice mattered? What are the ways that you ensure your voice matters when faced with injustice?

6. Aside from the promise made to his father, what is the importance of Max's retelling of the story of his family and his survival to new generations? How do stories from the past influence you and the choices you make in your life?

7. We live in a free and democratic society and are entitled to many basic human rights. Name some of those rights. What rights were taken away from Max and other Jews leading up to and during the Holocaust?

8. Elie Wiesel was another noted writer and Holocaust survivor. Like Max, Elie Wiesel survived in Auschwitz after losing many members of his family.

After the war ended, he also went on to speak about his experiences during the war. He once said, "Whoever listens to a witness becomes a witness." What do you think he meant by that? How does it connect to Max's life's work?

9. Righteous Among the Nations is a title that the state of Israel grants to those non-Jewish people who helped or saved Jews during the Holocaust. There is a garden in Jerusalem with plaques and statues dedicated to those who were named Righteous Among the Nations. Thinking about Max's life, who, in your opinion, might have been deserving of that title? What did they do to warrant that honour?